RENEWING BRITAIN'S RAILWAYS

Scotland

GORDON D. WEBSTER

AMBERLEY

This book is dedicated to my late grandfather and former railwayman
George B. Campbell (25 October 1924 to 22 October 2018).
'The Whiteinch Sha-a-dow'

First published 2019

Amberley Publishing
The Hill, Stroud,
Gloucestershire, GL5 4EP

www.amberley-books.com

ISBN: 978 1 4456 8921 0 (print)
ISBN: 978 1 4456 8922 7 (ebook)

British Library Cataloguing in Publication Data.
A catalogue record for this book is available from the British Library.

Typeset in 10pt on 13pt Celeste.
Origination by Amberley Publishing.
Printed in the UK.

Contents

Introduction

Scotland is home to some of the most beautifully scenic railways in the world, which draw in tourists from all countries. With an ever-growing population and an increasingly congested road network, the railways are now more important than ever to the country's economy, so modernisation is vital. The ScotRail passenger franchise was taken over on 1 April 2015 by the Dutch transport firm Abellio, while the Anglo-Scottish sleeper train contract was awarded to Serco, who assumed responsibility from the evening of 31 March. Previous franchisee First Group ran both daytime and sleeper operations. A more cooperative approach was adopted to manage Scotland's rail infrastructure, with ScotRail and Network Rail pooling their resources to form the ScotRail Alliance.

Faster, longer and more frequent trains are on their way north of the border, with the ScotRail Alliance overseeing numerous electrification projects in the Central Belt. A whole line was even re-opened in September 2015, with the relaying of part of the old Waverley Route from Edinburgh to Galashiels and Tweedbank. Furthermore, ScotRail are currently unleashing their own fleet of refurbished High Speed Trains (HSTs) to the public – otherwise known as InterCity 125s – with a spacious and comfortable modern interior that is so often lacking on today's railways. Abellio seized the opportunity when Great Western Railway (GWR) retired many of their HSTs from service and they will use the sets on expresses between Scotland's seven cities. The first refurbished Class 43 power cars and Mk 3 coaches have been outshopped in an attractive livery with the words 'Inter7City' featured on the bodyside – an inspired recreation of the popular InterCity brand used by British Rail (BR).

It is disappointing that Scotland's rural routes have never really been provided with the same promotion and world-class tourist facilities that adorn other scenic railways across Europe. Right at the start of the franchise, Abellio announced their commitment to achieving this, with their Great Scenic Railways of Scotland package. This initiative covers the West Highland, Kyle of Lochalsh, Far North, Borders, Stranraer and Glasgow–Carlisle via Dumfries lines. Refurbished trains and more luggage space were promised, along with onboard tourism ambassadors and much improved 'local produce' catering.

Almost four years later, most of the 'Scenic Railways' pledges have yet to be delivered. The main improvement has been the refurbishment of the ScotRail Class 158 DMU fleet: an interior refresh with more luggage space and new seating, in addition to far more table seats aligned with windows. But another great positive step was the ScotRail Alliance announcing they would fund a programme of lineside vegetation clearance over the next few years to open up long-lost scenic views for passengers on the West Highland and Kyle lines. Inspiration came from Friends of the West Highland Lines, who have coordinated tree-felling work for many years.

Unfortunately, in their first four years of the new franchise, Abellio ScotRail have been in the news all too regularly for the wrong reasons, with train punctuality at its lowest levels for years and cancellation figures unacceptably high. The situation became so severe that the Scottish Government issued the company with an eight-week improvement order in December 2018. Failing to meet their performance targets means Abellio could potentially be stripped of their ten-year contract earlier than planned. Frequent 'skip-stopping' by trains as a way of making up lost time has drawn widespread criticism and there are also frequent reports of overcrowding due to short-formed units, though this was a problem on Scotland's railways long before Abellio came on the scene.

The Forth Bridge became a UNESCO World Heritage Site in 2015 and the next few years will see a visitor centre established. A Turbostar DMU is seen crossing the famous cantilever structure above North Queensferry on 11 September 2018.

Poor performance also has financial penalties and ScotRail clocked up £1.6 million in fines during a three-month period in 2018 for failing to meet targets. A lot of the operator's difficulties seem to be rooted in staff shortages, particularly on the West Highland and Far North lines, with regular complaints about a lack of on-train catering. Even more concerning has been the number of cancellations on the Glasgow–Oban/Mallaig sections during the busy tourist season, often blamed on crew availability.

Serco's Caledonian Sleeper contract has not been without its challenges either, particularly locomotive issues, which I will look at later in this book. State-of-the-art new carriages are about to enter service, which bodes well for the passenger alongside ScotRail's new stock. I hope the photographs over the following pages give a good insight into both companies' operations during recent years. Freight traffic is another vitally important part of Scotland's rail future and I will also be covering developments in this sector.

The photographs included in this book have been specially chosen to show the wide variety of locomotives, multiple units and liveries to be seen north of the border during the last few years. It has been a rollercoaster period for the railway, which has ranged from the incredible (bi-mode Class 800 Azumas running over Drumochter Summit in the Highlands) to the farcical (a Class 66-hauled pipe train which took the best part of a day to get up the Far North line). No one can say it has been boring!

I also thought it fun to have a rover ticket-style tour of the country towards the end of the book as a means of displaying the pictures. Unlimited journey passes are the best way to get out and about on the railways and I would encourage anyone to make use of them if you get the chance.

GDW
Glasgow
January 2019

The End of Scottish Coal?

Just before the turn of the new millennium things were looking up for Scottish freight, when Transrail merged with Loadhaul and Mainline Freight to become part of English Welsh & Scottish Rly (EWS). EWS signalled their intention to revolutionise the trainload coal market with the introduction of the first 250 Class 66 locomotives (becoming sub-class 66/0) and over 1,000 new HTA hopper wagons. Traffic grew to the extent that a couple of long-closed branch lines in Ayrshire had their track relaid to transport coal from opencast mines at Broomhill (near Rankinston) and Greenburn (near New Cumnock). Broomhill would only last until 2002. Greenburn opened in 2004, as a spur off the existing branch to Knockshinnoch disposal point. The numerous opencast mines in Ayrshire were complemented by the intensive merry-go-round traffic from the deep-water port at Hunterston on the Firth of Clyde, conveying imported product from overseas. This was worked to the coal-fired power station at Longannet in Fife.

The push for greener energy would see the Ayrshire and Fife traffic gradually diminish from 2007 onwards, but the real death knell came on 1 April 2015, when the UK's carbon tax was effectively doubled in price. This resulted in the closure of most of Britain's remaining coal-fired power stations and the end of most Scottish coal trains. EWS had become part of DB Cargo by March 2016, when Longannet PS shut, and now Hunterston has ceased operation as a coal-loading terminal as well. The decline of the industry has resulted in significant job losses and the Stirling–Alloa–Kincardine route is now disused east of Alloa. A new railhead had been opened at Earlseat Mine, on the Methil branch, in 2012 and there were regular workings from here to Hunterston operated by DB. They too came to an end in 2015.

Ayrshire coal was generally transported from many old Scottish mineral railways south to power stations in England and Wales. Though the Beeching Report shut a lot these branch lines, several of them continued in freight use. One in particular is the former route to Dalmellington, which closed to passengers in 1964 but had a small deviation added to serve Chalmerston Mine. The 11-mile branch was mothballed in 2012. Traction-wise, Class 66s had a monopoly on all Scottish coals for a number of years, for EWS/DB, Freightliner and GBRf, though Freightliner Class 70s also made a few appearances from 2012 onwards.

Greenburn Mine lasted until summer 2018, outliving the neighbouring terminals at Knockshinnoch and Crowbansgate, New Cumnock. As of January 2019, the last remaining Scottish coal trains are workings out of Killoch washery.

The remote 3-mile branch to Greenburn opencast mine near New Cumnock often saw two return trains a day under operation by DB. EWS-liveried Class 66/0 No. 66009 is seen on 20 August 2014, leaving the loading site and beginning the twisting climb across the moors towards Bank Junction, where it will join the GSWR main line.

The wild nature of the Greenburn branch is well illustrated here, with GBRF Class 66/7 No. 66738 *Huddersfield Town* nearing journey's end while carrying empties from Tyne Coal Terminal on 7 April 2017. The gated Boig Road level crossing can be seen on the extreme left, with the town of New Cumnock behind.

Following loading at the terminal, the 66 in the previous picture is now seen rejoining the main line at Bank Junction, heading for Kilmarnock Long Lyes, where it will run round before heading back south in the same direction. At the time, GBRf usually worked one trip a day up the branch, but Freightliner had some traffic to Greenburn during 2018.

The GSWR main line was very busy with coal traffic on 25 March 2015, as power stations stockpiled supplies in advance of the new carbon tax. Class 66/6 No. 66623 *Bill Bolsover* was captured on an empty Carlisle–Hunterston working at Kirkconnel, sporting a unique blue version of Freightliner livery.

On the same day, a loaded Hunterston–Drax working passes The Cairn, on the 7-mile block section between New Cumnock and Kirkconnel. Heading the load is No. 66748, one of several 66s imported from the Netherlands, seen still in its original livery but with GBRf branding added.

The Killoch branch is holding on to what remains of Scottish coal traffic. Both Freightliner and GBRf have workings to England and South Wales, but these aren't guaranteed to run every day. A Freightliner Class 66 is seen here on an empty rake of HHAs, crossing the magnificent Enterkine Viaduct near Annbank.

The Longannet–Hunterston merry-go-round coal circuit used to see loaded or empty workings passing virtually every hour under EWS (latterly DB). By the time of this shot in April 2015 trains were fewer and mostly Freightliner-operated. The 66 is approaching Hunterston High Level for loading, with the Firth of Clyde in the background.

One of the DB-operated trains to Hunterston is seen at Ardrossan South Beach on 8 April 2015, in the hands of No. 66250, the very last of the 250-strong 66/0 sub-class. Introduced by EWS, the 66/0s dominated the Scottish coals for over fifteen years and were a regular sight at Ayr Falkland Yard and locomotive depot. In 1998 they began replacing the Class 37s, 56s and 60s formerly used.

Freight Focus

The loss of coal traffic has left a big hole in the Scottish rail freight scene and DB Cargo (formerly EWS) has lost further traffic flows as the company downsizes. This has paved the way for other operators to increase their foothold north of the border, particularly Colas Rail, who have taken over the ex-DB oil traffic, plus all cement workings, which were previously the responsibility of Freightliner.

Lengthy block trains are the key to survival for rail freight against an ever-growing trunk road network. The dualling of the A9 Perth–Inverness road is one of Transport Scotland's priority projects, making it harder for Highland Main Line freight to compete. However, major road construction projects in Aberdeen and Inverness have borne fruit for rail, leading to increased frequency of the cement workings from Oxwellmains, near Dunbar, for the raw materials. These very heavy trains require the most powerful locomotives such as Class 60s and these have in turn been replaced by Class 70s.

Longer trains running less frequently are more economical for the operators, with track access charges having to be paid for every train that runs. GBRf's North Blyth–Fort William alumina train was reduced from five trainloads per week in each direction to three, but now typically carries twenty-four tankers instead of a dozen. GBRf recently signed a new contract with Liberty Aluminium to last until 2022. One irregular flow that has operated for decades is the movement of large-diameter pipes from Hartlepool to Georgemas Junction on the Far North line. DB operates these on an as-required basis for North Sea oil activity. Each bogie flat wagon carries two or even three pipes, with additional 'runner wagons' required for extra space between as the pipes are over-length. Haulage is by a single Class 66/0. Recent runs during the leaf-fall season have seen the heavy train continually stall on the gradients north of Inverness, causing numerous delays and cancellations to ScotRail services. DB crews even had to sand the rails by hand on at least one occasion!

Scotland's roads are more congested than ever, but some help will be required if more goods are to be carried by rail. The Scottish Government has outlined its support for rail freight, recognising the vast environmental benefits, and has pledged to work with businesses to support its growth. More investment in the infrastructure will be needed however, as companies need assurances that trains will be fast enough and reliable enough to justify the cost. Reducing single-track sections and increasing the lengths of passing loops are required.

There are already sidings in place at many now disused railheads, which could be put back into operational use at minimal cost, such as J. G. Russell's Deanside Transit terminal in Glasgow. Walkers Shortbread is one of the biggest food exporters in Scotland and already uses trains to carry the goods. It is conveyed, among other containerised products, on a new DB-operated intermodal working which started in May 2018 between Mossend yard (near Motherwell) and Seaforth, Liverpool. Walkers uses lorries for the rest of the journey to its depot in Elgin. A journey by rail the whole way would seem more practical, with the potential for new sidings to be laid on the disused Elgin goods yard site.

A 2013 trial saw whisky conveyed from Elgin to Grangemouth, but nothing has happened since in this industry, despite numerous Scottish distilleries being adjacent to the railway, and some even still with sidings. The increasingly poor state of repair on rural Scottish roads is in part down to the heavy goods vehicles that batter them every day, conveying anything from whisky to metal and aggregates. In particular, the trunk routes through the Highlands are thoroughly congested during the tourist season, often narrow and twisting and completely unsuitable for trucks. The railways here have suitable capacity to take the strain away.

Highland Spring water is another UK market-leading company that has chosen to use rail and will hopefully inspire others. At the time of writing, a container terminal is being constructed at Blackford, to transport bottles from the firm's production plant in the Perthshire village, removing 40 per cent of lorry movements from the nearby road. This exciting development will see trains running daily along the Stirling–Perth line from Coatbridge Freightliner terminal, expected to carry a load of twenty-two containers, which would otherwise be twenty-two lorries a day. The disused station and goods yard at Blackford, accessed via the Up line, have been demolished to make way for the new sidings and container crane, while a new pedestrian footbridge will allow locals to easily cross the line instead of waiting at the existing foot crossing. With such a big investment, there is clearly confidence in the success of this scheme, with an expectation of traffic on the line for years to come.

There are many Scottish freight proposals which have yet to see the light of day, such as plans to reintroduce timber trains, last seen over a decade ago. There is the possibility of logs being loaded at Kinbrace on the Far North line once again and at Rannoch Moor on the West Highland line, but nothing concrete has been announced yet. Timber was previously carried in the Highlands as part of the EWS 'Enterprise' wagonload network. Mossend yard remains Scotland's major rail freight hub, but Millerhill, in Edinburgh, is generally now just used for civil engineers' trains.

GBRf, Colas Rail and Direct Rail Services (DRS) have become more established north of the border during the last few years and there has been a great need for infrastructure trains with all of the permanent way upgrades that have taken place: e.g. the Borders Railway construction and Edinburgh–Glasgow electrification. At Grangemouth, Colas works all of the oil traffic from the refinery despite a major closure scare in 2013, while

DRS and DB still operate container traffic from the WH Malcolm terminal and the docks respectively. The Grangemouth branch was electrified in 2018 as part of the Edinburgh–Glasgow Improvement Programme (EGIP), meaning the Anglo-Scottish freight can now be electric-hauled throughout.

DRS's introduction of Vossloh Class 68s in Scotland came in 2015 and they have since taken over the daily intermodal workings from Mossend to Inverness Needlefield Yard and Aberdeen Craiginches. The almost-identical fleet of ten Class 88s arrived in 2017 and now work the Mossend–Daventry containers. Where the 88s differ is their bi-mode capability, using OHLE pantographs to work under the wires and diesel engines for the non-electrified stretches. This allows them to work nuclear flasks such as the Sellafield–Hunterston working, going diesel for the 'last mile' or so to Hunterston Low Level terminal.

Colas have introduced Class 70s on much of the oil trains in lieu of Class 56s and 60s. However, fuel suppliers in the rural locations seem to prefer the logistics of road haulage and sadly the trains to Lairg and Fort William ceased in 2017. June 2014 saw the end of aviation fuel workings to Linkswood, near Leuchars, due to the closure of the RAF base, but the sidings at Prestwick Airport are still used. There are several other oil depots still rail-connected north of the border, but financial and logistical obstacles must be overcome if they are to ever see trains again.

Class 56s made a welcome return to Scottish lines in 2013, when Colas began using the type on aviation fuel traffic. On 12 May 2015, No. 56087 has just deposited a load at Prestwick Airport sidings and is seen passing Gailes golf links, 5 miles into its journey towards Grangemouth with the empties. Troon Harbour is in the background.

Hunterston B Power Station still provides nuclear traffic for DRS, despite the Ayrshire port ceasing to function as a coal-loading terminal. Early morning frost clings to the ground at West Kilbride on 25 March 2015 as Class 37 duo Nos 37604 and 37606 near their destination with three FNA flask wagons from Sellafield.

On a freezing 23 January 2013 it was the turn of heavily refurbished 37s Nos 37609 and 37605 on the Hunterston flasks. Taken at Motherwell, this picture shows the southbound working bound for Sellafield. Class 88s now usually work the flask traffic to Hunterston and Torness power stations.

DRS Class 88s are the first locomotives to work in Scotland using both electric and diesel power, their principal traffic being the Daventry–Mossend Tesco containers. On 16 August 2018 the northbound 4S43 speeds past Lamington with No. 88007 *Electra* up front. It has just crossed the River Clyde bridge, which was damaged in the 2015 storms.

Several miles further south on the WCML on the same day, No. 66709 *Sorrento* crosses the Clyde at the village of Crawford on the daily 6S50 Carlisle–Millerhill infrastructure train. The 66 carries the livery of shipping company MSC and has a light twelve-wagon load on this occasion, conveying ballast.

In April 2017 a landslip near Lambhill forced the closure of the Glasgow Queen St–Maryhill route for a week. Buses replaced West Highland trains all the way north to Crianlarich, though the North Blyth–Fort William 'bulks' still ran, diverted via Glasgow Central Low Level. On 6 April, the northbound loaded tanks are seen at Exhibition Centre station behind Class 66 No. 66737 *Lesia.*

Electrification to Cumbernauld and Stirling has encompassed the route via Falkirk Grahamston. This is Camelon, Falkirk, on 17 September 2015, before the wires went up. No. 66105 is heading empty flats; this a DB-operated flow, which conveys containers between the port at Grangemouth and Mossend.

EWS-liveried No. 66110 approaches Blackford with 6D83, the Aberdeen Waterloo–Mossend china clay tanks, on 17 September 2015. This working replaced a mixed freight in the timetable that used to be operated by EWS when wagonload workings were still commonplace.

Highland Main Line

The Perth–Inverness Highland Main Line has the potential to be a busy inter-city route, despite its long single-track sections through high altitudes among the Cairngorms. First constructed in 1863, a more direct route from Aviemore to Inverness was opened in 1898 over Slochd Summit, replacing its original course via Dava Moor and Forres. Double track was subsequently laid from Blair Atholl to Dalwhinnie and Daviot to Inverness, with the Perth–Stanley Junction section to the south being double-tracked too, as it was originally part of the Caledonian Rly's main line to Aberdeen via Forfar.

Expansion of the 118-mile route has always proved difficult due to the nature of the terrain and the infrastructure being set for single track. Nevertheless, an hourly ScotRail timetable is now on the way, made possible with the introduction of HSTs on services previously worked by DMUs. HSTs have been a daily sight for many years on the Inverness–London King's Cross 'Highland Chieftain'. Their use on the internal Glasgow Queen St/Edinburgh–Inverness workings will eventually allow for a ten-minute reduction on the journey time north of Perth, as the twin power cars of the 125 give greater acceleration compared to the Class 158s and 170s currently used. The use of HSTs by ScotRail has come about due to many of the class being made redundant by InterCity Express bi-mode Class 800s and 802s south of the border. Now refurbished and fitted with electric-powered automatic doors, the 125s are being introduced up north in shorter formations, with nine four-car sets and seventeen five-car sets making up the fleet.

Delays during refurbishment at Wabtec, Doncaster, and problems encountered during training runs have delayed ScotRail's introduction of HSTs into revenue-earning service. The first HSTs to arrive north for driver training were still in First Great Western blue livery but with logos removed and replaced by temporary ScotRail branding. Inverness depot will maintain the power cars and Mk 3 coaches along with Edinburgh Haymarket.

The new HSTs began full service on the Glasgow/Edinburgh–Aberdeen and Aberdeen–Inverness routes in December 2018. They were gradually introduced on Glasgow/Edinburgh–Inverness diagrams following the new year. Their introduction here will coincide with their replacement on the 'Highland Chieftain', as LNER (the new East Coast Main Line operator) will soon be bringing in its Azuma Class 800s. The bi-mode units are capable of running on diesel power to Inverness and some test runs have already taken place.

Transport Scotland has made commitments in the last couple of decades to upgrade the Highland Main Line and its timetable but changes have so far been minimal, with many highlighting the huge investments in the parallel A9 road in comparison. National transport campaigners have pointed out a promise made by First Minister Alex Salmond in 2008 that the Edinburgh/Glasgow–Inverness average journey time would be cut by thirty-five minutes by 2012, with only four minutes achieved so far, ten years later (but pre-HST). However, improvements should be possible with the re-signalling currently taking place at Pitlochry and Aviemore. Pitlochry's platforms have recently been extended and Aviemore's loop will be lengthened, which will be especially beneficial to freight trains.

The non-station, bi-directional passing loops at Moy, Tomatin, Slochd Summit and Kincraig offer a certain amount of flexibility on the Highland line, especially important with the hourly service soon to come. With an increased frequency, there is however more chance of a knock-on effect when one or two services are delayed on the single line. Increased double-tracking could be the answer – perhaps starting with the Culloden–Daviot section, which was singled in 1960 – but as always, this boils down to finance. The line has come a long way since the Beeching Cuts, when most of the double-track sections were singled and many stations were closed. The 1970s saw most of the double track reinstated, along with several crossing loops, when the North Sea oil boom brought extra freight traffic.

Class 60s had a relatively short tenure working over the Highland Main Line, operated by Colas from 2016 until 2018 when all the locomotives were sold to GBRf. On 1 June 2018, No. 60002 speeds through the bi-directional Up loop at Dunkeld while working 6H51, the 02.48 Oxwellmains–Inverness cement.

A healthy level of freight traffic is carried on the Highland Main Line today. Unlike the West Highland, the route has a relatively high line speed and adequate clearance for most modern container wagons to be used. The main goods flow is the Tesco intermodal train operated by DRS, running six days a week from Mossend Yard to Inverness and limited to a maximum length of twenty containers. Colas' cement workings from Oxwellmains run two to three times a week, while there is also traffic bound for the Far North. This includes occasional flasks transporting nuclear waste from the reactor at Dounreay and the DB pipe train, both running to the yard at Georgemas Junction. If even longer freights could be permitted there will be a stronger business case for haulage companies to use rail and get more lorries off the congested A9 road.

From a scenic perspective, the railway from Perth to Inverness is up there with the best in the UK. HSTs will bring a level of space and comfort ideal for tourist travel and this is something which the local service has been lacking since the mid-1990s. The line is well used by railtours and also the Royal Scotsman luxury touring train, which uses the main line connection at Aviemore to traverse the preserved Strathspey Railway. The eventual extension of the heritage line to Grantown-on-Spey will open up many more possibilities for rail travellers.

The daily Inverness–London King's Cross service – 'The Highland Chieftain' – has kept virtually the same timetable path since its introduction in 1984 under BR, using HSTs. On the evening of 6 July 2015 the 12.00 return from King's Cross rounds the curve into Dalwhinnie. The set is in an interim livery representing three different East Coast Main Line franchises from the past few years!

On 27 June 2018, Class 66/3 No. 66301 runs downhill past Dalnaspidal with 4D47, the 13.07 Inverness–Mossend empty Tesco containers. The temperature on this day touched 30 degrees Celsius at Dalnaspidal, some 1,400 feet above sea level. Supermarket supplies were first carried over the line by EWS for Safeway (to Georgemas Junction) following privatisation. DB used to operate the Tesco train before DRS took over.

For most of 2018 ScotRail drivers were trained on four-coach HSTs daily between Perth and Inverness, running empty but with station stops included. On the heatwave day of 27 June, power cars Nos 43021 and 43127 were captured heading south in Glen Truim, north of Dalwhinnie, still in First Great Western colours but with ScotRail branding.

On the evening of 27 June 2018 the same HST seen in in the last picture arrives at Pitlochry on its return working, where it will pass the 18.45 Inverness–Edinburgh ScotRail Turbostar. With resignalling in progress, the semaphores seen here will soon be a thing of the past.

Platform extension work is underway at Pitlochry on 9 November 2018, as the 10.45 Inverness–Edinburgh arrives. The 1911-built Highland Rly signal box is to be decommissioned in 2019 but should be safe from demolition as it is an A-listed building. The fine lattice post semaphore signal would be an ideal candidate for use at a preserved railway.

Steam on the Highland line, with new-build A1 Pacific No. 60163 *Tornado* climbing away from Carrbridge on 20 June 2015. This was one of several steam charters operated by Abellio ScotRail following their franchise takeover that April.

The double-track section from Inverness to Culloden once stretched as far as Daviot – reinstating this would boost capacity on the line. On 10 November 2018 the morning sun has yet to rise over the hill, as the northbound Caledonian Sleeper nears journey's end. No. 67003 is at the helm, in Arriva Trains Wales livery, and the location is near Daviot.

West Highland Line

If the West Highland line was a tourist attraction ten years ago, it is now surely a phenomenon, with its popularity growing year on year. Not only on the Mallaig Extension to the north – where steam haulage is now daily from spring to autumn – but on ScotRail services from Glasgow to Fort William and on the Oban line. The route's success has been partly down to support locally from bodies such as Friends of the West Highland Lines (FWHL) and The Highlands & Islands Transport Partnership (HITRANS), who are keen to make sure that the Scottish Government recognises key areas of improvement. The establishment of Community Rail Partnerships (CRPs) in Scotland is also now helping rural lines, with the West Highland CRP being formed in 2014.

Summer overcrowding has long been an issue in the West Highlands that has still to be properly addressed and the ScotRail Class 156 Sprinter fleet has now been in service for thirty years. Groups such as FWHL and the CRP argue that while the railway holds premier, worldwide 'tourist line' status, it lacks the imagination applied in other European countries for scenic journeys, where bespoke, spacious rolling stock and full catering facilities are commonplace. Current unit diagrams require Sprinters to shuttle between destinations in the Central Belt each day before or after working WHL services, to places like Alloa and East Kilbride. The onboard passenger experience is therefore, arguably, of the same standard as suburban commuters'.

An important breakthrough came in 2018 when Transport Scotland established the West Highland Lines Review Group to discuss a wide variety of potential service improvements on the railway. The involvement of stakeholders such as FWHL, the Lochaber Transport Forum and the Argyll & Bute/Highland Councils will ensure locals have a voice in how the timetable can be optimised and the rolling stock upgraded to serve the whole community better.

An early improvement was with the Sunday services, where traditionally there are certain trains which do not run in the quieter winter months. ScotRail announced that from March 2019, the Sunday Glasgow–Mallaig timetable would stay the same all year round, initially on a year's trial to test demand. This means there are now two through return workings between Glasgow and Mallaig instead of one, plus an extra Fort William–Mallaig return. The Review committee is also sure to discuss the large gap in the Monday–Saturday timetable of several hours without trains during the afternoon on the Crianlarich–Fort William section, where there are still only three Sprinters each way per day. The Glasgow–Oban section was doubled to six per day in 2014, to great success.

It is still unclear whether ScotRail will continue with its original plan to upgrade platforms and clearances on the West Highland routes for Class 158s to operate, or simply continue with 156s. Line speed and weight restrictions are still an obstacle and the Review Group will examine how these can be lifted. The Mallaig line has had no regular freight since 2005, and Oban since 2001, partly due to weak underbridges which prevent locomotives with a Route Availability any higher than RA5 from operating. This includes Class 66s, though they have worked on a 'special dispensation' basis with certain restrictions. The Orchy Viaduct on the Oban line is currently undergoing refurbishment; unrelated to this; one would hope opportunity might be taken to strengthen the structure for heavier locomotives.

In 2018, ScotRail announced that single-car Class 153 units are to be coupled to the 156 formations in the Highlands, converted for use as special bicycle and luggage vans. They are a type unfamiliar to the Scottish network and five of them have been cascaded from the south of England to cope with the extra demand and are expected to enter traffic in 2020. They will also include additional seating. It is also proposed the 153s will be trialled on the Far North and Kyle lines – another area where the trains are regularly used by campers and sports enthusiasts carrying bulky equipment.

Tree clearances in summer 2016 opened up stunning scenic views on the West Highland line at Morelaggan, overlooking Loch Long. Sprinter No. 156476 is seen passing on a six-car train bound for Oban and Mallaig. (N. McNab)

In recent years, many stunning scenic views lost to lineside vegetation have been opened back up with the tree clearance project led by FWHL. The first part of the scheme saw views recovered at Loch Awe and Glen Falloch, followed by Glenfinnan Viaduct. In 2016 a 350-metre section overlooking Loch Long, at Morelaggan, was tackled by the Network Rail/ScotRail Alliance, who committed to future clearances after seeing the huge success of FWHL's project. Two years later, magnificent views of Oban Bay were restored too, when shrubbery was cleared around the hill at Glencruitten Summit. It must be remembered, however, that overgrown vegetation is not confined to the West Highland lines, with routes all across the country being similarly plagued. Not only does this block views but it is a safety risk, especially during spells of high winds when trees fall on the track.

Another improvement on the West Highland routes has been the installation of the more reliable 'next generation' Radio Electronic Token Block (RETB) signalling, replacing the original system installed in 1988. A far more efficient railway would also undoubtedly be created by adding more crossing loops. Late-running trains on the long single-line sections often have knock-on timetable effects, such as on the 17 miles between Glenfinnan and Arisaig. This could be avoided by relaying Lochailort loop. Corrour has a hand-operated loop used only by engineers, and if this was brought into full-time use (at surely minimal cost) there could be big benefits.

One of the earlier tree clearance projects led by Friends of the West Highland Lines was at the north end of Loch Long, overlooking Arrochar village. This view shows the combined afternoon service from Oban and Mallaig climbing towards Glen Douglas.

Network Rail's Ultrasonic Test Unit (UTU) train makes regular visits to the West Highland line and other far-flung corners of the Scottish network. On the evening of 22 May 2015, Class 37/5 No. 37667 (now withdrawn) arrives at Arrochar & Tarbet while heading south. Colas now supplies traction for test trains instead of DRS (see page 67).

Many station buildings have been repainted into ScotRail's corporate blue and white from their traditional West Highland Railway colours – a very bold decision. Crianlarich, seen here, is one of the more dignified examples. Since this shot taken in 2014, stations have also had the First Group-era signs replaced with 'Scotland's Railway' examples and Passenger Information Systems have been added.

An engineer's possession south of Crianlarich on Sunday 3 March 2013 saw most West Highland services cancelled, as some jointed track was replaced. EWS-liveried Class 66/0 No. 66107 is pictured sitting stationary on the newly laid line near Glen Falloch atop a rake of JJA Autoballaster hoppers.

An SB Rail Plasser & Theurer tamper is pictured on the same day setting the new metal-sleepered, continuously welded track into place around the same location, just south of Crianlarich. See the old sections of jointed track on the right awaiting disposal.

After ballasting, Class 66/0 No. 66105 is on a second rake of JJAs passing County March Summit, on its way north to Fort William Junction yard. This area has many open, scenic views from the train, but a large new forestry plantation on the mountainside just south of Bridge of Orchy is a concern.

The West Highland line in winter, taken from the front cab of Class 156 DMU No. 156458, which is heading north. The train is about to cross the Horseshoe Viaduct near Bridge of Orchy, with the flank of Ben Dorain up ahead. The sign indicates a speed limit of 20 mph for locomotives and 30 mph for DMUs crossing the structure. (Reproduced with permission of ScotRail)

Coasting downhill on Rannoch Moor between Corrour and Tulloch, where the very sharp curvature of track is evident. This is the case over much of the moor, though there are sections of continuously welded rail that allow faster running – even up to 70 mph for Sprinter units on one particular stretch. (Reproduced with permission of ScotRail)

One of Network Rail's stoneblower machines takes a summer evening's rest in the sidings at Bridge of Orchy. These vehicles inject ballast beneath the rails to increase track stability.

GBRf Class 66/7 No. 66734 *The Eco Express* waits above Crianlarich station subway on 6S45, the 07.14 North Blyth–Fort William alumina 'bulks', on 26 June 2012. The very wet weather lasted all week in the West Highlands and was a sign of what was to come. Taking this routine snapshot, little was I to know that the locomotive had only two more days left in traffic...

The by-now tarpaulin-covered locomotive is seen seven months later alongside Loch Treig near Tulloch. It had in fact derailed two days after the previous picture, when it struck a landslip here hauling 6S45 and came to rest hanging precariously near the water's edge. The driver escaped uninjured but the 66 remained *in situ* for months. Recovery was so difficult that it took until summer 2013, when it was scrapped onsite! (Reproduced with permission of ScotRail)

Sadly West Highland oil traffic has ceased once again, after being briefly reactivated by Colas Rail. Class 66/0 No. 66101 is seen in the Scottish Fuels terminal at Fort William on 24 June 2014 after arriving with the weekly train from Mossend Yard, then operated by DB. The driver is disembarking after having shut down his locomotive. DB red was a livery not often seen on the West Highland line.

A misty summer's morning at Glenfinnan on 6 July 2015, with the 08.30 Fort William–Mallaig climbing the hill from the famous viaduct to the station. The leading Sprinter is in newer ScotRail colours with the rear one still in First livery.

The Royal Scotsman luxury train runs from Fort William to Mallaig and back on selected summer Saturdays. West Coast Railways (WCR) supplied the traction for several years but now GBRf has taken over using Class 66s. On 18 July 2015, WCR Class 47 No. 47854 *Diamond Jubilee* was leading the train into Glenfinnan heading back south. Class 37 No. 37516 was at the rear.

The 'Scotsman' is scheduled to pass the 08.21 Glasgow–Mallaig service at Glenfinnan on its way back to Fort William; the latter is seen arriving with Sprinter No. 156450 leading. The 47 and its train are too long to fit in the crossing loop here so the rear end is fouling the points. Therefore the 156 must wait until it has departed so the line ahead will be clear. The 'Scotsman' is also too long for Mallaig loop, hence why locomotives work top and tail.

The West Highland Mallaig Extension is still the place to see Britain's only timetabled steam-hauled trains, on the 'Jacobite'. On a wet 24 June 2014, LMS Black Five No. 45231 was making spectacular sound effects climbing away from Glenfinnan with the morning train. In contrast, the heatwave summer of 2018 resulted in many trains being diesel-hauled and the coaching stock suffering from excessive tyre wear.

As of early 2019, the Pass of Brander on the Oban line still has its unique 'Anderson's Piano' system of semaphore signals which protects the railway against rockfalls. Oban-bound Sprinter No. 156474 is pictured approaching Falls of Cruachan halt on 30 October 2015. The signals and their connecting trip wires are earmarked for possible replacement by fibre optic cables.

Serco Caledonian Sleeper

Anglo-Scottish sleeper trains remain a very attractive travel option amid a difficult economic climate and the competition from a range of low-cost airlines. The longstanding tradition of being able to fall asleep in London's busy metropolis at night before waking up to sunrise in the Cairngorms is the main selling point of the Highland sleeper, the colloquial name given to the nightly service (Saturdays excepted) from London Euston to Fort William, Inverness and Aberdeen. The three different portions of the sixteen-coach train continue to join and split at Edinburgh Waverley in the small hours, being diesel-hauled north of here. The Lowland sleeper runs from Euston to Edinburgh and Glasgow Central, joining/splitting at Carstairs. With the trains now operating under a standalone franchise separate from ScotRail, there have been various operational changes, with GB Railfreight (GBRf) now providing the drivers and traction, taking over from DB Cargo (formerly EWS).

The winter of 2015/16 – the very first for new franchisee Serco – was a challenging period thanks to the weather, which caused the closure of the West Coast Main Line (WCML) between Glasgow and Carlisle. Floods caused damage to the Clyde Viaduct at Lamington in late December 2015 and as a result, many WCML trains were re-routed via Dumfries on the Glasgow & South Western main line. This lasted for seven weeks until the WCML reopened on 22 February. The Highland sleeper ran for some of this period via the East Coast Main Line (ECML), using London King's Cross, while the Lowland sleeper went diesel-hauled via Dumfries. Various Anglo-Scottish freights also ran regularly via the GSWR route while engineers worked round the clock to repair the Clyde Viaduct. Virgin introduced a temporary Glasgow–Carlisle shuttle service using Voyagers.

The inauguration of the new Caledonian Sleeper (CS) franchise in 2015 saw Serco promise a major revamp of the rolling stock. £150 million is being invested in new Mk 5 carriages for use on the service, to completely replace the BR Mk 2s and Mk 3s used since the early 1980s. At the time of writing the Mk 5s – built by CAF in Spain – are being tested north of the border and based at Polmadie depot. Inverness depot will be responsible for their regular maintenance once they are in service. Their state-of-the-art interiors will include en suite toilets for the first time and a 'club car' with proper catering facilities to replace the current microwave ovens. The first batch of Mk 5s arrived in the UK in January

2018 following gauging trials in the Czech Republic. Their planned introduction to service in 2018 has been delayed until June 2019.

The biggest surprise following the new franchise concerned the locomotives. Serco announced that a batch of Class 73 electro-diesels would be specially refurbished into a new sub-class – Class 73/9 – for the diesel-hauled legs of the train north of Edinburgh. The locomotives had never previously worked in Scotland and, as such, concerns were raised over their suitability, most notably by the drivers' union ASLEF. The locomotives had in fact spent their careers working on the former Southern Region of BR, alternating between third rail DC electric power and their 600 hp diesel engine.

The 73/9s were gradually introduced into traffic in late 2015, resplendent in the new CS 'midnight teal' livery. A completely rebuilt cab front with new lighting was notable, with a new MTU 1,600 hp engine providing power. February 2016 saw the sub-class first used on revenue-earning service, following testing and some early empty coaching stock runs. Various faults over the following months saw them drift in and out of traffic, mainly related to their alternators. By November all six of the CS 73/9s (Nos 73966–971) had been introduced but they were rarely all in service at the same time, with locomotives often sidelined at Brush Traction, Loughborough, for repairs. By late 2016, common practice on the sleepers was Class 73 and Class 66 double-headers, with the 73s coupled inside just to provide heat and electricity, such was the extent of their problems. The 66s were hired in from GBRf and worked on all three legs, to Fort William, Inverness and Aberdeen.

The following year, most of the problems on the 73/9s had been ironed out and they have since become regulars to Fort William and Aberdeen. After early trials on the Inverness leg, that portion has reverted back to Class 67 haulage for the time being, with the locomotives once again hired from DB. Double-headed 73/9s are expected to feature over the Highland Main Line due to the gradients, while the West Highland and Aberdeen legs are usually operated by just single locomotives.

As if this wasn't enough variation already, Class 47 haulage is not unknown on the Scottish sleepers these days – truly incredible given the type was officially replaced on the diesel-hauled legs back in 2001. The big Type 4s have been used regularly by GBRf for empty coaching stock runs but traction shortages have seen them out on the big stage once again. The highlight came in early 2016, when a pair of 47s were booked to haul the Lowland sleeper each night from Glasgow Central to Carlisle (via Dumfries) and back again the following morning while the WCML was closed. Serco is still finding use for 47s in late 2018 – a position cemented when No. 47727 was repainted in CS colours and given the name *Edinburgh Castle*.

For the electric-hauled sleepers south of Edinburgh and Glasgow, GBRf began supplying Class 92s in 2015, though their appearances have been somewhat limited due to reliability issues. As a result, their predecessors, the Class 90s, have still been used, hired from DB and Freightliner. The AC Locomotive Group have also been providing locomotives to help since 2015: namely, preserved Class 86s Nos 86101 and 86401, plus No. 87002, the last operational Class 87 in Britain. All three are painted in CS colours, with all the necessary certificates and safety equipment to allow them to haul the services from Euston to Glasgow/Edinburgh, though they are generally preferred for the empty stock workings at Euston and Glasgow Central.

Sixteen coaches remains the maximum permitted load for any sleepers due to the platform lengths at London Euston. One notable change from 2016 was the increased load on the Fort William portion; the train's popularity saw it go from being normally four coaches to five and then six. The extra Mk 3s were available after the Aberdeen portion had its load cut, with passenger numbers in the Grampian region sadly affected by the decline of the North Sea oil job market.

With the help of various local transport groups in the north, Serco is looking at possible options to expand the current CS operations. One suggestion is to run a connecting overnight train to Wick and Thurso, with connections for Orkney. Oban could also be re-added to the Anglo-Scottish sleeper network, having lost its service back in the 1960s. Engineering work on the West Highland line in February 2016 saw the Fort William portion diverted to Oban at weekends, with 73s working the train top and tail. This allowed Serco to test the market and logistics of working to the Argyll town, which would be ideal for the ferry connections to the Hebrides.

The inauguration of the new Caledonian Sleeper franchise in 2015 saw No. 67004 painted in the new 'Midnight Teal' livery and given the name *Cairn Gorm*. On 24 June 2015 it worked 1Y11, the northbound service to Fort William, and is seen arriving at Arrochar & Tarbet. West Coast Railways' No. 37516 was dead at the rear of the train, heading back north after working the previous night's 1B01 to Edinburgh – an incredibly rare feat after years of 67 haulage on the West Highland portion.

2015 was the final summer of Class 67s on the Fort William sleeper. No. 67007 carries standard EWS livery in this shot taken at Crianlarich around 10 p.m., hauling the southbound service on a wet 5 July 2015. This locomotive was one of four 67s fitted with special iron-steel composite brake blocks to make them suitable for the gradients of the West Highland line.

The only other 67 to be painted in CS colours was No. 67010, which did not carry RETB equipment and therefore stuck solely to the Aberdeen and Inverness portions. The locomotive was captured at dusk near Culloden on 22 June 2015, heading the 20.45 Inverness–London Euston working (1M16) into the night. Not many Mk 2 or Mk 3 carriages received the new livery and there are only two in this rake.

67s were still working the Inverness sleeper in 2018 and for a number of days in May and June, it was Royal Train-liveried No. 67005 *Queen's Messenger* that did the honours. Early in the morning of 1 June, the Type 5 arrives at Dunkeld & Birnam with the northbound 1S25 to the Highland capital, passing the historic semaphore signals and Highland Rly box, which will soon disappear.

Few would have ever imagined the possibility of Class 73 electro-diesels working Scottish sleepers but the type is now standard north of the border. On 14 July 2016, Nos 73966 and 73968 are awaiting departure at Fort William on the 19.50 departure for Euston (note the InterCity-liveried brake coach). Despite being double-headed, the train ended up running over an hour late, as No. 73966 continually shut itself down on the approach to Spean Bridge.

Autumn 2016 saw GBRF Class 66s frequently piloting 73s on the Fort William sleeper. A view from the window on 1 November 2016 finds No. 66739 *Bluebell Railway* up front alongside No. 73967, crossing Rannoch Moor. This is almost a throwback to the days of steam on the West Highland line, where double-heading was standard practice, with the leading loco traditionally always the 'train engine' and the rear one the 'assisting engine'.

The same double-headed pair are seen later in the day, stabled with the stock at Fort William station. The normally freight-only 66s performed well on the sleeper and it arrived at Fort William bang on time that morning, despite it being the first train of the day during leaf-fall season, with rail conditions not at their best.

The Sunday 1M11 Lowland sleeper bound for London Euston awaits its 23.15 departure time from a quiet Glasgow Central on 27 January 2019. At the business end is Class 92 No. 92028, in GBRf livery.

Preserved Class 86 No. 86101 *Sir William A Stanier FRS* is seen at the buffer stops, having hauled the 92's coaches into Central from Polmadie depot. CS 'Midnight Teal' is arguably the smartest livery to be carried by this electric class in its fifty-plus-year career.

Edinburgh–Glasgow Electrification Part I: Queen St Diversions

For many years, the Edinburgh to Glasgow main line via Falkirk and Linlithgow has been ScotRail's flagship route. The 1950s introduction of Inter-City DMUs was ahead of its time, then superseded by a return to loco-haulage with the fast and frequent push-pull services of the 1970s and '80s. Always a busy commuter line connecting Scotland's two major cities, journey times were gradually slashed and more of the public bought into the rail revolution following privatisation, avoiding the M8 motorway as it became more congested. A fifteen-minute frequency followed, with ScotRail's Class 170 Turbostar units able to operate in either three or six-car formations. Rapid growth on the route pushed even this service to the limit and the short platform length at Glasgow Queen Street station was the main factor for six coaches being the maximum length allowed.

Electrification would be the next piece of the jigsaw to come, part of a wider programme titled the Edinburgh Glasgow Improvement Programme (EGIP). A Scottish Government priority project, delivered by Network Rail, EGIP would be a wider programme including the electrification of the main line north to Stirling and Dunblane, plus the Falkirk Grahamston loop and Stirling–Alloa, the latter of which had reopened to passengers in 2008. Using new purpose-built Hitachi Class 385 EMUs, the goal is to achieve a fastest journey time of forty-two minutes from Edinburgh to Glasgow. The initial budget for the scheme was £742 million, but it has soared considerably.

The Edinburgh & Glasgow Railway opened in 1842 and electrification – starting in 2016 – would be the biggest engineering project on the line ever since. The biggest part of the project would be the refurbishment of Glasgow Queen Street terminus to fit overhead catenary, replace the track and signalling and extend the platforms to allow eight-coach electric trains. 1.8 km of concrete slab track would need to be replaced in Cowlairs Tunnel within the station throat, so the trackbed could be lowered to fit the wires.

For this, a lengthy full closure of Queen Street was required, from 20 March until 6 August 2016 – a total of twenty weeks. All ScotRail services were diverted during this period, with the majority taking a circular route through Glasgow's low level system. Trains called at Queen Street Low Level station, sharing the line with the usual North Clyde electric services. It was an unprecedented and unusual exercise, seeing Class 156s, 158s and 170s work under the wires across the city, either in a clockwise 'east to west' or anti-clockwise 'west to east' direction, without the need for reversals.

As part of the diversion programme, the former crossover and junction at Anniesland (Knightswood South Junction) was rebuilt, which allowed the un-electrified Maryhill branch via Kelvindale to once again join the North Clyde line. The branch had originally re-opened in 2005, but without a main line connection. Following this, diverted trains from Edinburgh, Alloa and Dunblane would take the route from Cowlairs to Maryhill, Anniesland and Partick to reach Queen Street Low Level. After terminating, a new service would leave from the same platform to the north, tunnelling under the city via Bellgrove and Springburn to rejoin the normal route at Cowlairs. Some workings took the same circuit but in the opposite direction and Queen Street Low Level Platforms 8 and 9 became a hive of activity.

Southbound West Highland services would also run via the low level west to east, taking their usual route to Westerton but then to Anniesland and Partick. Northbound departures were via Bellgrove. Glasgow–Inverness/Aberdeen workings, on the other hand, used Glasgow Central station, as did a few Dundee and Perth locals. Central was accessed via Cumbernauld and Rutherglen – another unusual route.

The Queen Street diversions ran smoothly throughout, despite having to be squeezed into the intensive North Clyde electric timetable. Extra dwell time was provided for northbound trains stopping at Bishopbriggs to give room for possible delays but this proved overgenerous in the end, with many of the Stirling and Alloa-bound trains often seen waiting at the signals.

Normality returned on 6 August 2016, when the now-electrified Queen Street High Level reopened, a day ahead of schedule. However, this was only the first phase of the terminus' regeneration, as work is still ongoing to extend Platforms 2–5 beyond the buffer stops. A larger concourse is being built, stretching further onto the street at George Square, to cater for the predicted growth from a current 20 million passengers a year to 28 million by 2030. A new glass frontage is being built, carefully incorporated into the listed Victorian train shed. The magnificent James Carswell-designed arches were previously hidden from view at the George Square entrance for many years, but demolition of some disused buildings during the rebuild has revealed them once again.

On 14 April 2016, Turbostar No. 170417 arrives at Glasgow Queen St Low Level with an Alloa service, diverted from its usual route out of the high level terminus. As of 2019, all 158s and 170s have been repainted into Saltire colours, but the First ScotRail livery seen here survives on a few 156s.

Sprinters pass at Anniesland on 2 August 2016. The diverted 08.57 Oban–Glasgow Queen St is led by First-liveried No. 156474, while No. 156442 is in the bay platform with one of the ordinary Anniesland–Queen St shuttles via Kelvindale. The West Highland service is taking the main line from Westerton to Anniesland, as opposed to the Edinburgh trains, which were diverted via Kelvindale.

The newly laid crossover at Knightswood South Junction, where a connection was eventually laid to connect the main line to the Maryhill branch at Anniesland station. Two 158s are negotiating the pointwork onto the branch with a service bound for Alloa on the same day as the previous picture.

Rare track for ScotRail Turbostars Nos 170414 and 454, which are seen coming off the Maryhill branch at Anniesland on 2 August 2016. No. 170414 is in a special livery celebrating the new Borders Railway. It is an Edinburgh–Glasgow service and will stop at Queen St Low Level before continuing east back to the Scottish capital, via Bellgrove and Springburn.

Under the normal timetable Hyndland is one of Scotland's busiest through stations, but diverted DMUs were still able to pass without disruption. On 2 August 2016, Saltire Turbostar No. 170458 was paired with a First-liveried classmate, seen approaching with another Edinburgh–Glasgow train.

14 April 2016 sees No. 156485 pass through a busy Partick station on the 14.41 Oban–Glasgow. Until 2016 DMUs were very rare on this section of the low level route, but they are now used on regular empty stock diagrams, which allow drivers to retain route knowledge for future diversions.

Again taking the anti-clockwise diversionary route east from Anniesland to Queen St Low Level, a pair of Turbostars pass Yorkhill, with the Riverside Museum and Clyde Expressway visible alongside. It is once again a train from Edinburgh and the date is 14 April 2016.

On 14 April 2016 there was still a lot of track and platform rebuilding work to be done at Glasgow Queen Street. A freight train at the terminus is a rare sight indeed; this rake of wagons appears to be transporting waste materials as all of the permanent way is replaced in advance of overhead wires being erected.

The 2016 diversions also saw Class 170s working out of Glasgow Central for the first time, as Aberdeen and Inverness services terminated here. This scene shows No. 170401 awaiting departure for Aberdeen alongside two Class 390 Pendolinos (date unrecorded). Note the missing front coupling panel on one of the 390s.

Edinburgh–Glasgow Electrification Part II: The E&G Goes Live

The first major engineering blockade as part of EGIP was the work in Winchburgh Tunnel during 2015, which ran from 13 June to 27 July. The 360-yard tunnel – between Linlithgow and Haymarket – was closed to allow the trackbed to be lowered for overhead wires and this resulted in bus replacements east of Linlithgow. Dunblane–Edinburgh trains took the Winchburgh Triangle to Dalmeny Junction, where they reversed to get through to Haymarket and Waverley.

Electrification of the Edinburgh & Glasgow line was preceded in 2014 by the wiring of the Glasgow–Cumbernauld route. The E&G was supposed to be electric-ready by December 2016, but the work would not be totally finished for another year. Meanwhile, that month saw Edinburgh Gateway station open on the Haymarket–Dalmeny side of the Winchburgh Triangle, where an interchange was provided between trains and Edinburgh Trams heading to the city airport.

Another tram-train interchange is at Haymarket, which had a £25 million rebuild from 2012 to 2013. The new glass concourse is around ten times larger than the original station building and a wider new footbridge has the usual refinements such as escalators and lifts. At Edinburgh Waverley, Platform 12 was extended by 75 metres to accommodate eight-car formations of the new Hitachi Class 385 EMUs for the route. The platforms at intermediate stations Croy, Falkirk High, Polmont and Linlithgow were also extended for the same reason.

Overhead wiring of the E&G was complete by mid-2017 and September saw it energised. The first electric train to haul passengers was on 10 December 2017, using Class 380 EMUs Nos 380113 and 380020. 380s – normally found on the Clyde coast lines out of Glasgow Central – began to be used on an interim basis, initially working one train per hour alongside Class 170 Turbostars, which still were still used on the majority of diagrams. The plan was originally for the new Class 385s to work the route from the outset, but with big delays at the production plant, it soon became clear they would be nowhere near ready in time.

The bulk of the Class 385 EMU fleet is being built at Newton Aycliffe, Durham – sixty-three sets to be exact – though the first seven were assembled at Hitachi's Kasado plant in Japan. When finished, there will be forty-six three-car sets, classified as Class 385/0. The remaining twenty-four sets will be four-car Class 385/1s, making it a total fleet of seventy units. The 385/0s are standard class only but the 385/1s have a first class section in one saloon. Pairs of 385/1s working in eight-car formations will become standard once the platform extension work at Glasgow Queen Street is complete. The increased train lengths will boost Glasgow–Edinburgh service capacity by up to 44 per cent at peak times compared to Class 170s. Their improved acceleration will achieve the forty-two-minute journey time. To maintain the 385s, a new depot has been built on the site of Edinburgh's Millerhill yard.

The 385s use regenerative braking, which reconverts energy back into the overhead power supply. This will help to lower the railway's carbon footprint along the E&G, as well as the usual benefits afforded by the traction change from diesel to electric. As well as the Edinburgh via Falkirk trains, 385s will also eventually be deployed on other lines in central Scotland once they are all delivered. This should include Glasgow–Edinburgh via Shotts, Glasgow–Edinburgh via Carstairs, Glasgow–Edinburgh via Cumbernauld, Glasgow–Falkirk Grahamston, Edinburgh–North Berwick, Edinburgh–Alloa/Dunblane and Glasgow–Alloa/Dunblane. Their introduction will also lead to mass diagram reshuffles for other classes of DMU and EMU, including the withdrawal of Class 314s. Eventually, some other Strathclyde suburban routes will also see 385s, namely Lanark, Neilston and Cathcart Circle workings out of Glasgow Central.

Capable of 100 mph running, the Gourock and Wemyss Bay lines were used as a night-time testing zone for the first couple of 385s, which arrived north in early 2017. However, drivers' union ASLEF raised concern of a 'fishbowl' effect when viewing signals from the cab, due to the smaller-than-normal curved windscreens. In other words, during training it appeared to drivers as though they were seeing two or three signals up ahead instead of one. This issue meant the units would miss their next expected introduction date of March 2018 and the completed sets were sent away for modifications to their windscreens.

New, flat windscreens were subsequently fitted to all of the 385s starting in spring 2018, but there were more problems at the factory which delayed the units' entry into service again, this time software faults. Class 380s continued to work the E&G but many of the Class 170 DMUs they were working alongside were due to be taken off lease, as ScotRail had signed a deal to transfer sixteen units to Northern Rail. This was part of the mass unit cascades planned on the back of the introduction of 385s and the HST. With the delivery of both classes well behind schedule, ScotRail had to find an interim measure to avoid a severe rolling stock shortage.

This was largely solved by a temporary deal for ScotRail to lease ten four-car Class 365 EMUs from Govia Thameslink Railway, lasting until May 2019. Part of the Networker family of units, the 365s had until then spent their entire careers in South East England, where locals nicknamed them 'Happy Trains' on account of their 'smiling' cab-front appearance. It was happy news for Edinburgh–Glasgow commuters once they entered service on the line in June 2018, normally operating in pairs as eight-car formations, giving a much-needed capacity boost. The ten Networkers retained their Great Northern white base livery, but had doors painted dark blue and ScotRail logos added as an interim scheme. The class had to be gauge-cleared before they began operation and subsequently the first couple of units were brought up north by road.

The 365s were soon joined on the E&G by the first couple of 385s – now passed for revenue-earning service – in July 2018. In August ScotRail was able to finally start operating an all-electric service, with a mixture of 365s, 380s and 385s. More 385s have been entering traffic since on a gradual basis and as of January 2019 around half of the class are at work (a mix of three and four-car units), with the rest to be delivered by the end of the spring. With sufficient cover on the Edinburgh–Glasgow services now, this has allowed 365s and 380s to be freed up for other lines. 380s have been used on the Glasgow Queen St–Falkirk Grahamston services (now Glasgow–Edinburgh via Cumbernauld), having started in July 2018 after the line between Polmont Junction and Larbert was fully wired. Most of the 365s then took over Edinburgh–Dunblane workings that December, working in four-car form – with Dunblane now the northernmost limit of standard-gauge electrified line in the UK.

The Edinburgh & Glasgow line in April 2013, pre-electrification. First ScotRail Barbie-liveried Turbostar No. 170459 passes the site of Waterside Junction, near Lenzie, on a Glasgow-bound train. This is one of the units now working for Northern Rail.

Pairs of Class 380s covered many of the Edinburgh–Glasgow services from 2017 to 2018 until enough 385s were introduced into traffic. Normally more associated with Ayrshire and Inverclyde, this is No. 380111, seen exiting the tunnel at Falkirk High. The Victorian-era stonework contrasts vividly with the modern overhead catenary – something which sums up the scale of the job to upgrade the 1842-built Edinburgh & Glasgow Railway to modern standards.

The new order at Falkirk High on 11 September 2018, as Class 385/0 No. 385005 leads a seven-coach train for Edinburgh while paired with a four-car 385/1. There were only a handful of 385s in traffic at this point, and services on the line were still shared with 365s and 380s.

The Class 385/1s all carry first-class accommodation at one end, such as on No. 385104 seen here. This is denoted by the yellow band and number 1, which is a nice throwback to BR days. 385s carry 'Express' branding too, while HSTs are 'InterCity'. No. 385104 has the modified windscreens, implemented after the original design of the glass caused signal sighting problems for drivers.

No. 385104 is captured in full flight heading a seven-coach Glasgow–Edinburgh train near Polmont on 11 September 2018.

Southern Networker EMUs in Scotland – a sight few would have ever imagined. On 11 September 2018 this pair of Class 365s were captured crossing the Avon Viaduct near Linlithgow on an Edinburgh–Glasgow service.

Colas Rail Class 37/4 No. 37421 heads an Autoballaster train across the Avon Viaduct a few minutes later, heading for the West Highlands. This slow-moving freight spent (as scheduled) several hours laying over between three different passing loops on its long way west!

By late 2018, electrification had spread to Dunblane and 365s took up the Edinburgh–Dunblane diagrams. Taken on 4 January 2019, we can see here why the units are known as Happy Trains! No. 365521 sits at Dunblane on the 11.00 departure south (which terminated at Haymarket) while No. 365529 has just arrived on the 09.51 from the Scottish capital.

That same morning, No. 365509 waits at Dunblane on the 10.28 to Edinburgh as a ScotRail HST, led by power car No. 43147, thunders past on the 09.39 Glasgow Queen St–Aberdeen. The HST is an unrefurbished 'classic' set. At this time, only a handful of 125s had entered passenger service and they mainly worked the Edinburgh-Aberdeen circuit, plus the odd Glasgow working.

Glasgow Queen Street, 25 January 2019. The terminus is now fully electrified and No. 385110 is heading a seven-car formation for Edinburgh, taking up almost the full platform length. Note the new signal gantry, plus another 385 to the right at Platform 3. Queen Street's refurbishment is still ongoing.

Scottish Signalling Revisited

Scotland is still a major stronghold for mechanical signalling at the time of writing, but won't be for too much longer. My previous book *Signal Boxes and Semaphores: The Decline* detailed the major resignalling plans by Network Rail to have virtually every British line controlled by new Regional Operating Centre 'control room'-type offices within the next few years. Manual signal boxes (most of which date back to the pre-Grouping era) and semaphore signals are being decommissioned, largely making way for LED colour lights and track-circuited sections of railway, with a long-term aim of having the whole of the country controlled by in-cab signalling, known as the European Train Control System (ETCS).

Two years after the original book project, it seems a good time to revisit the Scottish signal boxes and see what progress has been made. Some of the surviving boxes are over 140 years old now, some considerably refurbished but most retaining the fine architecture and character of the pre-Grouping companies. Forres was a 1896 Highland Rly (HR) design, sadly demolished with resignalling between Nairn and Elgin in late 2017. This was in part to allow an extended crossing loop and track deviation at Forres, with a brand-new station being built. Nairn–Elgin is now controlled by the 'Highland Workstation' at Inverness Signalling Centre, with axle counters fitted to the track for train detection, i.e. Track Circuit Block (TCB). Elgin's 1951-built box (formerly Elgin West) has also been demolished. This scheme has also brought an end to the single-line Key Token working from Aberdeen to Inverness. Exchanges at Nairn were done from the station building – this has also come to an end.

Aviemore and Pitlochry will be the next HR boxes to close, during 2019, with the rest of the Highland Main Line boxes possibly closing in stages between 2021 and 2024. As with all resignalling schemes however, it depends on Network Rail's budget and could be delayed. Indeed, the Stirling–Perth line was slated for 2016 but the boxes here could still have a future for a few years yet. Blackford is one example, the 1933-built LMS cabin still being required for now to give access to the new Highland Spring water terminal. The increase in both passenger and freight frequency along this stretch will also mean a return for Greenloaning box, which has by and large been switched out of use for over a decade. Network Rail began recruiting new signallers to work here in 2018 and its reopening will break up the long Dunblane–Blackford section and allow extra trains. The passing loops and crossover have recently been disconnected though, deemed to no longer be required.

Despite electrification at Dunblane the box has survived, though most of the station area now uses LED colour lights. There are a couple of semaphores near the north end however, which look quite incongruous next to the overhead wires! A similar situation exists on the freight-only Grangemouth branch, where Fouldubs Junction box is still in place. But on the main line, the EGIP electrification saw Carmuirs East and Larbert North shut in 2018.

The busy Perth–Aberdeen route is still largely semaphore-controlled using Absolute Block working, which also stretches towards the boxes at Tay Bridge South, Leuchars and Cupar in Fife. The situation also remains unchanged on the GSWR main line, with boxes and semaphores at Lugton, Mauchline, New Cumnock, Kirkconnel, Thornhill and Holywood. All these aforementioned locations in the north-east and south-west are expected to hold on to their manual signalling for at least another five years.

Most GSWR boxes on the Ayr–Stranraer route should also have a few years left. There is even a plan to refurbish the obsolete Key Token instruments from the Aberdeen–Inverness line and fit them on the Stranraer line, to replace the slightly older Tyers No. 6 tablet machines. It is the last railway in Britain to feature Electric Train Tablet working, between the boxes at Girvan, Barrhill, Glenwhilly and Dunragit (LMS-built, from 1927). There is no freight on the route and an infrequent passenger service south of Girvan, so trains passing on the single line are few and far between. Barrhill box could close soon as a result. Other boxes are at Kilkerran loop and Stranraer Harbour (normally switched out).

Forres signal box was knocked down in 2017 when the new station and crossing loop were built. On 20 June 2015, the signaller swaps the single line token with the driver of an Inverness-bound train – a century-old tradition which has now come to an end on the Aberdeen–Inverness line. (Photo taken with permission of Network Rail)

Elgin box (formerly Elgin West) was also demolished in 2017. While the Elgin–Keith section used Tokenless Block working, Elgin–Forres required Key Tokens to be issued to drivers as permission to occupy the single line. They were issued from this Tyer's Key Token instrument contained inside Elgin box. (Photo taken with permission of Network Rail)

While key token working on the Aberdeen–Inverness route has been eliminated, the remaining signal boxes on the east end of the route survive for now, using Tokenless Block apparatus. On 20 June 2015, a Class 170 passes Keith Junction box, which was built by the Great North of Scotland Rly (GNSR) in 1905. (Photo taken with permission of Network Rail)

The interior of Huntly signal box, which was built by the GNSR in 1890 and still surviving at the time of writing. There are twenty-five levers but those painted white are out of use. The blue cabinet above them in the middle is the electrically operated Tokenless Block instrument. (Photo taken with permission of Network Rail)

The 1898-built Aviemore box is expected to be closed by the time of publication in 2019, with control of the station area transferred to Inverness Signalling Centre. This is part of a major project to extend the crossing loop, with all of the semaphore signals being replaced by colour lights. The box is a B-listed building, so is unlikely to be demolished.

Of the remaining boxes on the Highland Main Line, Pitlochry will be one of the first to close, around the same time as Aviemore. This shot was taken in June 2018, prior to the platform being extended across the front. Like others on the route, it was refurbished in recent years and has a prominent extension containing a toilet.

On 9 November 2018, the 12.09 Glasgow–Inverness passes the semaphore signals at Kingussie. Platform 2, on the left, has been recently resurfaced. The box here should have at least a couple more years left before full resignalling of the Highland Main Line.

Mechanical signal boxes still dominate on the line from Dunblane to Perth. Auchterarder box (built 1895) survives despite the station here closing in 1956. Being quite a remote location, with the village located about a mile away, the station reopening would seem unlikely.

With so many boxes closing, it is nice to see one reopening. Greenloaning – normally switched out – will be reactivated in 2019 due to an increase in traffic. On 4 January 2019, a southbound Turbostar passes the box and the now-disconnected passing loops.

The Stranraer line sees sparse traffic nowadays and Barrhill box is likely to be the first to close, which will simplify operations. This tiny Glasgow & South Western Rly (GSWR) cabin houses the lever frame and the remote crossing loop is still guarded by semaphore signals.

Glenwhilly, 21 October 2015. The 14.43 Stranraer–Kilmarnock service approaches across the lonely moor as the signaller crosses the track to swap the single line tablet with the driver. Compare this with the 1988 photo on page 60 and note how much the Down starting signal is leaning twenty-seven years later!

The remaining boxes along the GSWR main line continue to use Absolute Block working as originally installed. New Cumnock is a prime example, having been built in 1909 and heavily refurbished. The faded and rusting Down starting signal seen here is one of the more interesting semaphores around.

1980s/90s Archive

The 1980s was the final decade of diesel-hauled passenger trains on most of Britain's railways, with most secondary routes being taken over by Sprinter DMUs during the period 1987–90. In Scotland, Class 150, 156 and 158 units largely replaced Class 37s and 47s, which had been the mainstay of traffic since the early 1980s. The 37s and 47s had themselves previously replaced Type 2 traction: Classes 25, 26 and 27. Sprinters also soon displaced most of the 'heritage' DMUs operating on local traffic, such as the Class 101s and 107s.

Even today it is still widely acknowledged that loco-hauled trains provided a level of space and comfort that Sprinters just cannot offer. The changeover was a backwards step in many ways, with a reduction in luggage space, panoramic window views and table seats for travellers. Astonishingly, rakes of five Mk 2 coaches on the Highland Main Line were downgraded to two-car 158s and a similar situation existed on other lines such as the West Highland, where the 156s simply could not cope with the tourist season demand. But Sprinters were more reliable and had quicker acceleration than loco-hauled trains. They would cut journey times and they would certainly cut costs for BR, requiring less maintenance and minimal shunting.

BR's ScotRail sector brought the curtain down on loco-haulage without ceremony or any special farewell runs and the following pages show some action from the final months. The Class 37/4 and 47/4 sub-classes covered most internal Scottish services latterly, being fitted with electric train heating (ETH), which replaced steam heat. The Glasgow–Carlisle/Stranraer workings in south-west Scotland were the first to see 'Sprinterisation', in October 1988, while 37-hauled West Highland services went over to Class 156s in January 1989. May 1989 saw 47s finish on the Aberdeen–Inverness route, followed in May 1990 by Class 47/7s on the Glasgow–Edinburgh/Aberdeen push-pull services. Finally, October 1990 saw the Highland Main Line go over to 158s – apart from the 'Clansman', the through train to London Euston. All Scottish sleeper trains remained loco-hauled as well.

The introduction of a full 156 Sprinter timetable on the Inverness–Wick/Thurso/Kyle of Lochalsh services was put off for several months after the River Ness bridge in Inverness was washed away by floods in February 1989. With the line to the north being cut off, six 37s and a number of coaches were marooned on the route and the new units couldn't get there by rail. A temporary measure saw 37s continue to work, with services terminating at Dingwall instead of Inverness. 156s eventually arrived by road and would take over most trains, though 37s were kept for one return train to Kyle in the summer months for the next few years. This used the special green and cream Hebridean Heritage tourist stock, which had an observation car.

Loco-haulage would return to most of the other scenic routes too over the following few summers, to ease the overcrowding on Sprinters. The period 1992–94 saw regular workings on the West Highland, Oban and Kyle lines, plus the Highland Main Line, largely using 37/4s but also 37/0s, as train heat was not required at that time of year. Privatisation brought these workings to an end.

With the ScotRail franchise being operated on a tighter budget than ever today, it looks unlikely that we will see much loco-haulage in the short term. The exception to the rule is the Monday–Friday commuter trains on the Fife Circle using Class 68s, though HSTs are of course taking over many internal workings also. The high leasing and operating costs of hiring locomotives and stock from other companies is one of the critical factors. Short platform lengths always ruled out loco-haulage returning to Glasgow Queen Street and then there is the general lack of run-round loops and the difficulty of shunting at terminuses such as Inverness.

The other side of the coin is the numerous benefits loco-haulage gives, with overcrowding on Scotland's railways seemingly worse than ever. The Caledonian Sleeper offers a quieter journey compared to travel on DMUs, without the noise and vibrations of underfloor engines, plus better scenic views from windows. Top and tail operation – with a locomotive at each end – is successfully used south of the border, but the hire and maintenance of an extra engine hikes up the costs. This is why the single-headed Fife operation works well, as the train works up to Glenrothes and back in a circular motion so the Class 68 arrives back at Edinburgh Waverley the same way around, without having to run round. Perhaps an arrangement could be made for these workings to run to other destinations at weekends, when the locomotives and stock would otherwise be out of use at Motherwell depot?

Large logo No. 37419 awaits departure from Kyle of Lochalsh on the afternoon service to Inverness, on 6 August 1988. This particular member of the class was very distinctive with its various front-end embellishments and decidedly dodgy right marker light, which seemed to afflict it for quite some time. Two more 37s were also at the Kyle out of shot: No. 37416 on the Hebridean Heritage stock (left) and No. 37414 on a railtour! (David Webster)

The February 1989 Ness Bridge collapse meant Class 37s had a stay of execution on the Kyle and Far North lines, with the introduction of Sprinters having to be delayed. On 24 April 1989, No. 37416 is seen at Dingwall, uncoupling from a train it hauled from the Kyle. Buses substituted for trains between Dingwall and Inverness during this period. (David Webster)

No. 37417 *Highland Region* (in InterCity Mainline livery) deputises for a Class 47 on the 09.33 Glasgow Inverness, climbing on the approach to Slochd Summit on 7 April 1990. Closer inspection of this photo revealed the driver has a few visitors in the cab! Whether or not they are operating personnel is unknown. (David Webster)

Generally, Class 47/4s ruled on the Highland Main Line until the October 1990 introduction of Class 158s. Another Inverness-based diesel, No. 47460 waits at Blair Atholl on 7 April 1990, hauling the 07.00 Inverness–Glasgow. Note the driver leaning out of the cab, waiting for the guard's flag before departing. (David Webster)

InterCity Mainline livery was essentially InterCity colours but without any logos, and another locomotive to carry it was No. 47595 *Confederation of British Industry*. It is seen at Gleneagles on 24 April 1989, hauling the 16.30 Inverness–Glasgow. The snow on the front suggests it was a wintry day on the higher ground further north, despite it being late April. (David Webster)

On a misty 5 September 1987, No. 47657 rumbles off the south end of the Tay Bridge at Wormit, hauling an Aberdeen–Edinburgh service. It is an interesting rake of stock, with four air-conditioned Mk 2 coaches and four Mk 1 BG full brakes, perhaps containing parcels or newspapers. (David Webster)

The ScotRail-liveried Class 47/7s were allocated to the Glasgow–Edinburgh/Aberdeen push-pull services but could be found on other routes too. On 5 September 1987, No. 47708 *Waverley* was captured in the rain at Leuchars station, hauling an Edinburgh–Aberdeen service. (David Webster)

SPT carmine and cream livery was preceded by Strathclyde PTE orange, which lasted until well after privatisation. It was carried by some of the Derby Heavyweight Class 107 DMUs, such as No. 107426, which was seen arriving at Leuchars on 5 September 1987 with a train for the south – well out of Strathclyde territory! (David Webster)

Loco-hauled trains offered a much larger capacity for bicycles and luggage on West Highland services compared to Class 156 Sprinters. On 17 October 1987, the 13.00 Oban–Glasgow Queen St was double-headed by Nos 37423 and 37413 *Loch Eil Outward Bound*, seen near Tyndrum Lower. A single 37 sufficed on most trains, so this was a fortunate shot. (David Webster)

For most of the 1980s Stranraer was still served by direct trains to and from London Euston – both a daytime working and an overnight sleeper. The Up daytime service – the 11.05 out of Stranraer – is seen arriving at Glenwhilly loop behind No. 47482 on 26 September 1988. This was during the last week of loco-haulage on the ex-GSWR routes (except the Euston sleeper) before the introduction of Class 156 Sprinters. (David Webster)

An undated photo – taken around 1990/91 – of Eastfield locomotive depot in Glasgow, shot from a passing train. Class 26s, 37s and 47s can all be seen, as well as an 08 shunter, in a variety of liveries. Eastfield closed in 1992 but was rebuilt for use by ScotRail DMUs in 2005. Overhead wires have now reached the depot from the line into Glasgow Queen Street, so EMUs can also be maintained. (David Webster)

SPT Daytripper

The Strathclyde Daytripper ticket has been around for many years, allowing unlimited travel by train, Glasgow Subway, buses and even some ferries for a day across the whole SPT (Strathclyde Partnership for Transport) network. This excellent-value 'scratchcard'-type ticket is only £12.70 for one adult and up to two children, or £22.50 for two adults and up to four kids, and is valid seven days a week at the time of writing. Covering all of Glasgow, one can also go west as far as Balloch then Ardlui on the West Highland line, while in the north-east it stretches towards Cumbernauld and Caldercruix. South of the Clyde, the boundaries are roughly Shotts, Lanark, Larkhall, Gourock and Wemyss Bay. It then takes in much of Ayrshire towards New Cumnock and also on the Stranraer line as far as Barrhill. Taking a virtual Daytripper journey of our own, we will look at the south-west corner of the country and some of the highlights to be seen...

The rails of south-west Scotland have always been underrated from a scenic point of view and tend to feature little in photographs compared to those in the north. The Stranraer line has now received some well-deserved recognition from ScotRail designating it one of their Great Scenic Rail Journeys, as has the GSWR main line (the Nith Valley) from Glasgow to Carlisle. The Clyde Coast routes have some spectacular views out to sea, with ferry connections to islands such as Bute and Arran.

The Inverclyde lines to Gourock and Wemyss Bay were the first in the country to be electrified too, outwith Glasgow. Gourock terminus – formerly of the Caledonian Rly – at least retains its original three platforms alongside the pier for ferries to Dunoon on the Cowal peninsula. The station fell into major disrepair after privatisation, with the main entrance building and glazed canopies being removed, eventually followed by the ornate metal supporting structure. A whole new glass-fronted building was added in 2010, followed afterwards by new platform shelters. Another big change at Gourock, in June 2011, was the frankly ridiculous decision taken to replace the Caledonian MacBrayne car ferries to Dunoon with the tiny, passenger-only Argyll Ferries.

Calmac ferries to Rothesay, on the Isle of Bute, connect with trains at Wemyss Bay station, which has retained its stunning Caledonian Rly architecture, unlike Gourock. The terminus was refurbished from 2014 to 2016 and work on the platforms meant it was unable to accommodate the Royal Scotsman for its usual west coast itinerary during summer 2015. As a result, the luxury train visited Gourock instead until the work was finished.

IBM halt on the Wemyss Bay line became the first station to close in Scotland since the 1980s, when ScotRail announced trains would stop calling there from the December 2018 timetable change. The station was essentially a private platform for workers at the IBM computer plant, which had itself shut a few years earlier. Patronage had subsequently become very low and anti-social behaviour had become a problem at the quiet halt (this is a notorious issue onboard Inverclyde trains in general, where a stronger British Transport Police presence would surely be welcome). ScotRail will continue to maintain the station however, with a view to re-opening if the nearby industrial estate is redeveloped.

Further south, an exclusion zone had to be set up at Ayr station in August 2018 when it was discovered that emergency repairs had to be carried out on the station hotel overlooking the platforms. The iconic building – constructed in 1866 by the GSWR – had lain disused for several years, gradually becoming run-down, and it was found there was a risk to the public of falling roof debris. The south end of the station had to be sectioned off, meaning the two through platforms – Nos 3 and 4 – were closed until further notice. The bay platforms – Nos 1 and 2 – were shortened in length so only a maximum of four coaches could fit. As a result, Glasgow–Ayr electric services had to be short-formed for some time.

The disruption was more severe still, as no trains were permitted to use the through lines to go south of the station. This included empty stock, with the result that ScotRail could not access Townhead carriage sidings to operate its normal timetable effectively. Services to Stranraer were cancelled completely for over two months and eventually some Glasgow–Ayr services started terminating at Prestwick Town to free up platform space at Ayr, while work went on to make the station safe again. 1 November 2018 saw some Stranraer services

Class 380 No. 380004 arrives at a much-rationalised Ardrossan Town station on 12 May 2015. Princes St level crossing (beyond the platform end) was previously an open crossing but had automatic half-barriers added in 2013. Network Rail is gradually reducing the number of open crossings in Scotland following an increased number of incidents in recent years, though most of them lie in the Highlands.

reinstated, before the full station at Ayr came back into use again on 20 December, though the bay platforms remain cut back for now due to the close proximity of the hotel. Demolition of the building is now inevitable, with little chance of it finding any profitable use.

The Glasgow-bound 380 leaves Ardrossan Town, with the superb sandy beach in the background. The other nearby level crossing is at Ardrossan Harbour, which was converted from an open type to half-barriers in 2012. South Beach station (seen earlier) also lies in close proximity.

Ardrossan Harbour is a simple one-platform terminus opened in 1987 to replace Ardrossan Winton Pier station. This shot from 14 August 2014 shows a 380 alongside the connecting ferry to Brodick, Arran. MV *Isle of Arran* is now a veteran of the CalMac fleet but is still required for relief sailings on her old route during the summer months.

Pioneer Class 380/0 No. 380001 awaits departure from Largs on 8 April 2015. The seaside terminus now looks rather bare. This is a consequence of the 1995 accident, when a train crashed through the buffer stops and came to rest on the main town street in the background, largely destroying the original glazed canopy and station building.

The sea wall at Saltcoats – on the Kilwinning–Largs route – is the most susceptible in Scotland to storms. Traffic consists almost entirely of Largs and Ardrossan Harbour services, which have been improved by the introduction of the quiet and comfortable Class 380s. When this shot was taken on 21 April 2015, coal trains to Hunterston still operated regularly too.

The southern end of Ayr station was closed off in August 2018 for several months due to the deteriorating condition of the station hotel above the platforms and the safety risk to passengers. In this 2015 view, terminating services from Glasgow and Girvan are seen side by side, while scaffolding surrounds the disused 1866 building, visible beneath the footbridge.

Train and combine harvester – a combination rarely captured in a photograph. This mid-summer scene near Howwood shows a Class 380 speeding north to Glasgow Central, past the local monument Kenmure Hill Temple.

The Daytripper ticket covers the GSWR main line as far south as New Cumnock, but this photo is taken several miles further on just to show the scenic splendour of the Drumlanrig Gorge. The train in question is the 12.13 Glasgow Central–Carlisle, seen rounding the S bends at Enterkinfoot on 25 March 2015.

The magnificent A-listed station concourse at Wemyss Bay was midway through a major refurbishment in this April 2015 shot. There is scaffolding at the platform ends and trains at Platform 2 were using a temporary buffer stop further back than usual. The Friends of Wemyss Bay Station look after the floral displays and run a bookshop at the terminus.

After many years'
absence, Class 318s are
starting to reappear on
the Inverclyde lines.
11 January 2019 sees
No. 318270 arrive at
Bishopton on the 13.57
Wemyss Bay–Glasgow
Central. The previous
day this unit
deputised for a Class
314 on the 13.24
Gourock–Glasgow.

Motherwell station is
served by a mixture
of local ScotRail
traffic, including
Glasgow low level
and Lanark services,
with Platforms 1
and 2 also used by
WCML expresses. On
27 October 2017, a
northbound Statesman
Rail charter makes
a stop at Platform 2,
hauled by West Coast
Railways' Class 47
No. 47826.

Network Rail's
Plain Line Pattern
Recognition (PLPR)
train visits many
destinations through
the night when there
are no public services
running. At 1 a.m. on
21 March 2018 it waits
at Balloch, before a fast
run back east through
Glasgow's low level
system. It has Colas
Rail Class 37s in charge:
No. 37099 *Merl Evans
1947–2016* leading and
No. 37421 on the rear.

Glasgow Roundabout

The best way to explore Glasgow's railways is with a Strathclyde Roundabout ticket – a day's unlimited travel at the absolute bargain price of £7.20 per adult (at the time of writing). It does cover a large chunk of the Strathclyde network further out too, so one can go as far as Dalreoch, Cumbernauld, Motherwell and Barrhead. Unlimited use of the Glasgow Subway is also permitted.

Recent years have seen a lot of investment in station upgrades within Glasgow, with more disabled-access facilities added, such as new footbridges incorporating lifts, and resurfaced platforms. Old First ScotRail and SPT-coloured buildings and signage have been upgraded to ScotRail Saltire, while more digital passenger information systems have been added to give real-time arrival updates. There was a considerable push to get many upgrades done in time for the 2014 Commonwealth Games in the city, such as the heavy refurbishment of Dalmarnock station on the low level Argyle line.

All traction depots in Glasgow are now used for EMU maintenance as well as diesel units, with ScotRail operating out of Eastfield, Yoker, Shields Road and Corkerhill. Virgin West Coast and Caledonian Sleeper rolling stock is maintained at the former LMS shed of Polmadie.

Meanwhile, Glasgow Works – an institution of locomotive building and maintenance for over a century – is sadly facing closure soon, unless an eleventh-hour deal can be found to save it. Originally the Caledonian Rly's major manufacturing headquarters, the St Rollox plant was subsequently downsized through the years, becoming British Rail Maintenance Limited (BRML) Springburn, then going through various owners after privatisation. Knorr-Bremse bought the site from Railcare when it survived a closure threat in 2013 and it has subsequently passed to Gemini Rail. Glasgow Works was responsible for a considerable amount of ScotRail unit overhauls in recent years, including Class 156s, 314s and 320/3s. More refurbishment contracts have started to go elsewhere, with the Wabtec Rail sites at Kilmarnock and Doncaster converting the newer 320/4s. 180 jobs are expected to be lost if St Rollox finally closes its doors.

Glasgow Works was also responsible for the last major overhaul given to Glasgow's Subway units, with the 1992-built trailer cars visiting Springburn in 2007. The current Subway stock will be replaced by new driverless trains designed by Stadler, which are expected to enter service in 2020. Around £300 million is being spent on them and other modernisation to Glasgow's 10.5-km underground line, including the refurbishment of every station. Smartcard ticketing has now been introduced and there is work taking place to upgrade the track, tunnels and signalling. The Subway celebrated its 120th anniversary in 2016 and this saw two of the power car vehicles painted in special colour schemes. No. 101 carries the original blood and custard Glasgow District Subway Co. livery, complete with vinyls representing the old cage-type doors. No. 130 carries a modern silver scheme, based on the new colours that will be carried by the driverless units. The contemporary livery on most vehicles is SPT orange and silver.

Guided tours of Glasgow Central station are now a regular event, allowing the public to explore the Victorian passageways hidden beneath the platforms. The demand for the tours so far has been overwhelming. On 28 November 2013 it is just another busy weekday at The Central, as both two-car and four-car ScotRail Sprinters arrive simultaneously from the south.

Two brand-new platforms were added to expand Central station in 2010, built over the former platform-level car park. They are seen occupied on 16 June 2015 by No. 380021 and the now-withdrawn No. 314212, while Network Rail's New Measurement Train – a refurbished HST – awaits departure on one of its occasional visits.

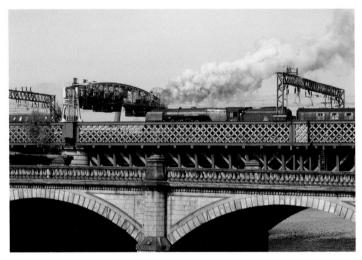

An awesome sight, as preserved Duchess Pacific No. 46233 *Duchess of Sutherland* powers away from Glasgow Central on 4 May 2017, crossing the River Clyde. She is heading towards Carlisle with the 'Great Britain X' railtour.

Oops! Polmadie depot on the morning of 11 January 2019 and it appears one of the Class 08 shunters has derailed; staff can be seen attempting to get it back on the track. On the right the Lowland sleeper stock is being shunted, with No. 92028 on the rear, having hauled it overnight to Glasgow Central.

February to March 2018 saw the heaviest snowstorms in Strathclyde for years, with a Red Alert weather warning and numerous line closures. Ironically, the West Highlands were affected little in comparison. On 3 March, after the blizzards had subsided, a four-car Sprinter was captured heading south at Pollokshields East.

On 19 September 2018, gale-force winds brought one of Scotland's busiest routes to a standstill at Partick. The overhead wires were damaged and ended up dangling over the road outside the station, with workmen sent out to direct traffic away. A Class 334 can be seen here stranded up above with passengers onboard, while the roof of a 318 can also be picked out.

2012 saw a large new footbridge – complete with lifts – built at Hyndland station on the North Clyde line. Not only is the station now disabled-friendly, it gives better local access for residents, especially to Gartnavel Hospital. On 31 October 2012 it was still under construction, with a Milngavie-bound Class 318 passing.

Network Rail test trains formerly used Class 31 power. On 23 October 2008, FM Rail's No. 31459 *Cerberus* sits in the passing loop at Hyndland, about to propel its two-coach load away on a tour of Glasgow's low level lines. A DBSO push-pull unit is at the other end.

With the exception of a few Class 314s, the popular Strathclyde carmine and cream livery has now become a thing of the past. When this shot was taken at Jordanhill on 23 January 2013, ScotRail's EMUs were in the midst of the repainting programme into ScotRail Saltire colours. Nos 318252 (left) and 334001 both carry different variants of the old livery; note how the 334s had a turquoise stripe.

The current Glasgow Subway units are due to be withdrawn and replaced by driverless trains in 2020. Power car No. 101 was repainted into original blood and custard livery in 2016, to celebrate the underground railway's 120th anniversary. It is seen leaving Shields Road on 16 January 2019.

The Spirit of Scotland

The mother of all rover tickets is the Spirit of Scotland travelpass, formerly called the Freedom of Scotland. This offers unlimited travel across all of Scotland's railways for a period of any four days (out of a consecutive eight-day period) or eight days (out of fifteen consecutive). As of January 2019, ScotRail have reduced it in price by 20 per cent in a 'winter sale', bringing it down to just £111 for the four-day ticket or £143 for the eight-day ticket; they are normally £139 and £179 respectively. As with the other rover tickets, child versions are also available. Sleeper trains are not covered by the Spirit of Scotland (except for the 04.50 Edinburgh–Fort William seated portion) but all other train companies are, in addition to Caledonian MacBrayne and Argyll Ferries, the Glasgow Subway, Edinburgh Trams and selected bus services. It gives further discounts on other transport such as preserved railways and can be used to cross the border on trains as far as Carlisle or Berwick-upon-Tweed. More information about the Spirit of Scotland – and all other rover tickets mentioned in this book – can be found on the ScotRail and SPT websites.

Travellers will notice newer ScotRail Saltire station nameboards across the network today and there are more than ever with Gaelic names printed below. This policy has even extended to Breich on the Glasgow–Edinburgh via Shotts line, which is one of Scotland's least-used stations, with an average of just three passengers a week in the 2015–16 period. The wayside halt was potentially facing closure in 2017 following a consultation by the Scottish Government. It was subsequently reprieved in November of that year and was refurbished the following summer, with the platform length and height adjusted for future electric services.

The Shotts line was fully electrified by late-2018 and EMUs are set to begin work imminently. A fifth electrified route from Glasgow to Edinburgh has now been opened up as well, with Glasgow–Falkirk Grahamston via Cumbernauld services now being extended eastwards. Replacing the previous DMU services, they now continue via Linlithgow on the E&G route to reach the Scottish capital, running half-hourly. This was one of several brand-new services introduced in the December 2018 ScotRail timetables. Class 318s and 320s continue to work Milngavie/Dalmuir–Cumbernauld services via Glasgow Central Low Level, meaning all stopping trains on the route via Greenfaulds are now EMU-worked.

The introduction of so many new services and new trains north of the border in the last few years has sparked a major reshuffle of unit allocations and route diagrams. After many years of predictability, some routes can now throw up a variety of traction, especially with delays in the new rolling stock being delivered and other classes having to cover elsewhere as a result. 2010 saw the first big changes with the new Glasgow–Edinburgh railway via Airdrie and Bathgate opened and Class 320/3s largely moved from the North Clyde low level route to the Argyle line. Over the next few years they began operations out of Glasgow Central High Level to Lanark along with 318s. 2011–13 would see them overhauled at Wabtec Rail, Doncaster, when they were fitted with toilets and repainted in Saltire livery. Surprisingly, the 320/3s retained their SPT-style seating covers after this. But these are now finally being replaced, with a follow-up internal refurbishment now underway, to add power sockets among other refinements.

Unit availability on Glasgow's low level lines was boosted when ScotRail leased seven former London Midland Class 321s during 2016. These four-car units were reduced to three cars and renumbered as Class 320/4s, with the first three still carrying London Midland colours when they entered service in March of that year. Eventually, all seven were refurbished and given Saltire treatment. A further five ex-Class 321s were ordered in 2017 to bolster the fleet and these are currently in the process of being released from Wabtec, Kilmarnock, after refurbishment as 320/4s.

The mass reorganisation of ScotRail unit allocations has been chiefly down to three factors: the introduction of HSTs, Class 385s and other routes going from diesel to electric power. It has had a domino effect, complex and far-reaching, and will ultimately lead to the withdrawal of the elderly Class 314s. As well as the sixteen departing Class 170s, electrification has led to five 156s and eight 158s leaving to join the Northern Rail fleet. ScotRail's remaining 156s are now being refurbished and fitted with toilet retention tanks, new seating, power sockets and accessible toilets among other things, in a similar fashion to 158s. Previous 156, 158 and 170 turns to Falkirk Grahamston and Alloa now use Class 380s and 385s. Class 365s are expected to continue on the Edinburgh–Dunblane services until their lease to ScotRail ends in May 2019.

Class 380s have spread onto other routes in 2018, such as the Cathcart Circle, including to Newton and Neilston. These routes also regularly produce 318s and 320s, as well as the 314s until they are withdrawn. Even the Inverclyde routes have thrown up some surprises in the latter half of 2018, with 318s now becoming semi-regular on Wemyss Bay services and occasionally to Gourock – lines they were displaced from back in 2011.

The first ScotRail HST service was on 15 October 2018 with a refurbished set working an Edinburgh–Aberdeen–Dyce diagram. With the 'Inter7City' conversions well behind schedule and ScotRail keen to get some sets into traffic before Christmas, the December timetable change saw several 125s start work still in GWR condition. Currently, around a dozen four-car HSTs are at work for ScotRail in total, based at Haymarket depot. Their initial movements have been unpredictable, mainly working Edinburgh–Aberdeen, but also many Glasgow–Inverness/Aberdeen services and 'over the top' from Aberdeen to Inverness. ScotRail designated the unrefurbished HSTs 'Classic' sets and left special instructions to customers about how to correctly use the slam doors (power slide doors were expected to be the norm by this stage).

The first couple of months of ScotRail HST services were dogged by cancellations as not all crews were fully trained in time. This was not an ideal time for disruption either, with not only the festive period underway, but also a big service increase, including the Glasgow–Edinburgh via Cumbernauld workings. December 2019 is to see big enhancements in the Grampian region as part of the Aberdeen–Inverness Improvement Project. Local Inverness–Elgin services are to become hourly and Aberdeen–Inverurie half-hourly, possible with the single track east of Inverurie being re-doubled. So far, most of the double track has been reinstated and preparations have been made to build new stations at Kintore and Dalcross (for Inverness Airport). One of the major undertakings is a £10 million investment to divert the A96 road onto a new overbridge at Inveramsay on the Inverurie–Insch section, to replace a narrow underbridge.

Resignalling on the west end of the Aberdeen–Inverness line and the deviation at Forres was the first phase of the line upgrade. The line was originally built on a straight east–west alignment at Forres, but the arrival of the Highland Rly with its main line over Dava Moor in 1863 required a new triangular interchange station to be built and the existing line took a loop to the south slightly to join it at that time. The straight east–west section was kept as a goods avoiding line, but eventually closed. To improve efficiency and speed up services, it was decided to relay track over roughly the same formation as the avoiding line and cut out the kink to the south during 2017. The existing station was then closed and an all-new one was built on the new formation.

Year-on-year growth means Virgin's Glasgow Central–London Euston timetable is now hourly – or greater. On 16 August 2018, an eleven-car Pendolino sweeps through the Clyde valley near Crawford, on the 13.40 from Glasgow. This service runs under a Class 1 (express passenger) headcode: 1M14. Several Euston trains run via Birmingham and are classified as Class 9 headcodes.

The new alignment at Forres is 1.5 km long, with LED colour light signals replacing the semaphores and a much longer 'dynamic' loop laid. There are two platforms now, replacing the previous one, and the nearby road now heads above the line on a bridge, replacing the old level crossing. A large new car park has been built and landscaping has covered the site of the old station. New Forres opened on 17 October 2017, with all trace of the old formation now removed. Meanwhile, the existing station at Elgin was refurbished and the old goods yard vastly scaled back, with removal of the overhead container crane. Both Elgin and Insch had platforms lengthened to accommodate HSTs.

The Far North and Kyle of Lochalsh lines north of Inverness will – like the West Highland line – retain their radio signalling (RETB) for the foreseeable future. These lines are similarly restricted and prone to long delays because of a lack of passing places. The busiest section from Inverness to Dingwall was once partly double-track and Friends of the Far North Line are keen for the loop at Lentran to be relaid to improve operations (it was lifted in 1988). Conon Bridge station has been a great success in the area since it was reopened in 2013, albeit on a single track. Its short and basic platform serves an important purpose in the nearby village, built at minimal expense. Hopefully this will be a good template for many more rebuilt stations to follow across the country in the coming years.

A CrossCountry Voyager threads its way north through the countryside near Auchengray, on the Edinburgh–Carstairs route.

Class 320/3s have now become regulars on the Cathcart Circle in Glasgow's south side. On 6 October 2018, No. 320309 approaches Mount Florida on a Glasgow Central-bound service.

One of the first batch of ScotRail Class 320/4s pauses at Exhibition Centre station on 6 April 2017. The 320/4s are converted London Midland Class 321s, transferred north of the border to boost capacity around the Strathclyde network. This particular unit, No. 320415, was the first of the new sub-class to be fully refurbished and repainted in Saltire livery, entering service in August 2016.

Breich is one of Scotland's (and Britain's) least used stations and until recently, only one train in each direction stopped here every day. Surviving a major closure scare, it has been refurbished as part of the Glasgow to Edinburgh via Shotts line electrification. On 19 April 2014, No. 156439 is seen speeding non-stop towards Edinburgh, while No. 156456 is waiting on the evening stopping service to Glasgow.

The Shotts line is now fully electrified but one diesel-hauled diagram set to remain is the daily ECS runs between Motherwell depot and Edinburgh, which form the Fife Circle loco-hauled services. On 12 October 2018, No. 68016 *Fearless* heads the afternoon eastbound working through West Calder. This shot was taken from the new footbridge, which had to be built to allow room for the electric wires.

Above: The morning/evening Class 68-worked diagrams on the Fife Circle are ScotRail's only loco-hauled services aside from the recently introduced HSTs. No. 68007 *Valiant* is one of two 68s painted in ScotRail colours to match the Mk 2 coaches, and is seen on 11 September 2018 coming off Jamestown Viaduct on the 18.17 Glenrothes–Edinburgh.

Left: No. 68006 *Daring* (also in ScotRail colours) rumbles off the north end of the Forth Bridge on the second loco-hauled diagram, working the 17.19 Edinburgh–Cardenden on 11 September 2018. These six-coach trains help to alleviate rush hour overcrowding on the busy Edinburgh–Fife section.

The Fife loco-hauled workings initially used Class 67s and stock hired from DB. On 10 October 2013, No. 67030 leaves Edinburgh Waverley on the 17.08 Fife circular service, with engine and coaches both in EWS livery. Using locomotives frees up DMUs for strengthening other services, such as the 158 seen on the right.

Platforms 5 and 6 at Edinburgh Waverley are being extended for use by Class 800 Azuma EMUs, while No. 12 has been lengthened for Edinburgh–Glasgow electrics. The existing Class 91s that work to London King's Cross will be made redundant once sufficient Azumas are in traffic. This November 2013 shot shows No. 91122 arriving at Waverley's east end.

Stirling is another station now changed forever with electrification. This scene from 17 September 2015 shows it before it went under the wires, but after most of the semaphore signals were removed two years earlier. Freightliner's No. 66550 is heading empty coal hoppers from Longannet through Platform 9, while a ScotRail Turbostar is waiting to head north.

On 25 February 2016, an Aberdeen–Glasgow service crosses the South Esk Viaduct beside Montrose Basin. There is still a 2-mile single-track stretch from Montrose to Usan, which could perhaps be doubled to increase capacity on the Dundee–Aberdeen line.

The Aberdeen–Inverness line now takes a more-or-less straight course through Forres at the new station opened in 2017. Before this, the track had a kink to the south to reach old Forres station, located on a sharp curve. On 10 November 2018, Class 170 No. 170414 calls at the new platforms, coupled to a Class 158. The Turbostar has lost its special Borders Railway vinyl livery, seen earlier.

The same train leaving Forres and the new deviation is apparent at this point. The position where the line changed course is where the fences are. The track now curves in from the left foreground back onto the original formation, whereas it previously curved in more sharply from the right.

Taken from roughly the same position in June 2015, when Forres signal box (built 1896) was in place and the crossing loop was much shorter. The same lorry depot and security fence on the left of the previous picture can just be picked out in the distance. The new line has been built in to where the bushes are.

Conon Bridge station was re-opened in 2013; it was originally just known as Conon prior to closure in 1960. Lying between Inverness and Dingwall, it is served by both Kyle and Far North line services. It is now a simple one-platform halt, only long enough for one coach, meaning the guard of each train has to operate selective door opening.

The Kyle line is another one of the 'Great Scenic Railways' advertised by ScotRail and funding has been set aside for lineside vegetation clearance similar to the West Highland. As daylight fades on 10 November 2018, the 12.08 Kyle of Lochalsh–Inverness arrives at Garve, one of the crossing points on the route.

Class 314 Farewell

The sixteen Class 314 EMUs are now the oldest traction in the ScotRail fleet and should all be withdrawn from service once sufficient Class 385s have been released into traffic, allowing other units to be cascaded in to take their place. The three-car electrics – built by BREL, York, in 1979 – were expected to be extinct by the time the writing of this book was complete, but delays to the new trains have given them a stay of execution. By the time you are reading this, however, the 314s will likely be gone forever.

The writing was on the wall for the class after their last overhauls were completed from 2011 to 2013, with many emerging from Glasgow Works still carrying old SPT blood and custard livery and still not equipped with CCTV, being the only ScotRail units not to be. Just five 314s were repainted in ScotRail blue, but all got a full interior refresh with Saltire seating. Hopes of a heritage repaint were dashed when the run-down of the class started in September 2018, though it is hoped Abellio will arrange a special farewell for them when the time comes.

Into 2019, 314s have remained concentrated on largely the same routes as recent years, if not quite as numerous now. All are routes out of Glasgow Central High Level: to Cathcart (inner and outer circles), Newton, Neilston, Paisley Canal, Gourock and Wemyss Bay. The type is not so popular in Inverclyde and has even frequently made the news, with locals slating the draughty saloons and lack of toilets, particularly problematic on the all-stations 'slow' trains, though ScotRail has latterly employed them on the 'fast' workings. Another older feature is the onboard PA system, with announcements still read out manually by the drivers.

Nos 314207/212/213 were the first members of the class to be withdrawn, in September 2018, but Nos 314207 and 213 were subsequently reinstated just two weeks later due to stock shortages. No. 314212 has certainly worked its last train, being taken to Glasgow Works on 9 January for component recovery, and as of January 2019 Nos 314201/204/206/213 are now stored at either Shields Road or Yoker depots.

No. 314213 leaves Glasgow Central on a Newton service as No. 314214 comes in from Paisley Canal on 28 November 2013. Note how No. 314213 has a First Group logo on its cab, as this was before Abellio won the ScotRail franchise.

A morning rush hour scene on 17 June 2015, as No. 314216 leaves Central on a Cathcart Outer Circle service, passing an empty Pendolino which will form the next departure for London Euston. By this time, the carmine and cream-liveried 314s were completely unbranded, with no First or SPT logos.

When this shot was taken on 25 January 2019, Class 314s were living on borrowed time and their workings had become unpredictable, with 318s, 320s and 380s covering many diagrams. No. 314208 is arriving at Central's Platform 7 with the 13.19 Newton–Glasgow. It was one of five units to receive ScotRail Saltire livery.

Class pioneer No. 314201 was stored just after Christmas 2018 and has likely worked its last train. On 3 March that year, the unit was captured arriving at Pollokshields East on a working off the Cathcart Circle, following heavy snowfalls. The 314s were actually purpose-built for the Argyle line through Glasgow Central Low Level, but shifted to lines out of the High Level after privatisation.

Mount Florida on 6 October 2018. No. 314204 (left) is on the 15.35 Glasgow–Neilston, while a six-car formation of Nos 314202/211 (right) is arriving on the 15.28 Neilston–Glasgow. The December 2018 timetable change saw 380s take over most of the Neilston workings and six-car 314s have since become rare.

No. 314211 is seen leading No. 314202 this time earlier the same day on the 14.35 Glasgow Central–Neilston, captured at Whitecraigs. The roller-blind destination boards are a dated feature, while the units also have emergency end doors fitted on the cab fronts, for tunnel operation on the Glasgow low level lines, which they worked earlier in their forty-year careers.

The Inverclyde lines have been a stronghold for 314s in recent years. On 21 May 2015, No. 314206 waits to leave Gourock on the 12.54 slow train to Glasgow Central. Its last passenger working was the 13.24 ex-Gourock on 23 November 2018, before it was subsequently stored at Shields Road depot.

The driver of No. 314205 checks the automatic doors are clear prior to departure from Bishopton on 11 January 2019, working the 13.55 Glasgow–Gourock fast train. The unit looks very run-down and appears to have been vandalised, but with most of the graffiti now removed. 314s are the last class to carry SPT carmine and cream livery, which originally appeared in 1997.

A much smarter No. 314214 is pictured at Paisley Gilmour Street on the 13.50 Glasgow–Gourock fast train on 25 January 2019. Eleven of the original sixteen sets remain in traffic at the time of writing. Will they see out the spring of 2019?

Return of the Waverley

The closure of the 98-mile Waverley Route from Edinburgh to Carlisle on 6 January 1969 is generally regarded as one of the biggest mistakes of the infamous Beeching Report. Fully opened by the North British Rly in 1862, it was one of the principal Anglo-Scottish main lines, but due to its topography it abounded with sharp curves and steep gradients, meaning journey times were lengthy. Deemed unprofitable by the powers that be, the entire line was lifted south of Millerhill yard in Edinburgh. This left a large part of Scotland cut off from the rail network, with only bus transport over relatively poor rural roads.

Campaigning to reopen the northern section of the route gathered pace in the 1990s and, after surveying the abandoned trackbed, the Waverley Railway (Scotland) Act was passed in Parliament in 2006. It was revealed that the relaid line from Edinburgh to Tweedbank, near Galashiels, would be christened the Borders Railway, with construction eventually starting in April 2013. A full length reopening to Carlisle was out of the question, with the main aim to reinstate some much-needed transport links to Galashiels and the villages to the north, partly for commuters to Edinburgh. For decades, the Borders was the largest region in Britain without a railway station.

For most of the route, the relaid Borders Railway follows the old formation. Little of the trackbed had been built over in the intervening years; one deviation was at Galashiels, where redevelopment of the town meant a newer station had to be built slightly further north. The twenty-three-arch Newbattle viaduct near Newtongrange had stood the test of time and was refurbished, but a new 87-yard concrete-span bridge had to be constructed at Hardengreen, with new road schemes built around it. The disused Stow and Gorebridge stations were essentially brought back into use on the same site as before, but Eskbank and Newtongrange were relocated slightly from their old locations. Shawfair is a new station on another deviation of the old route. Tweedbank is also new, having been chosen to be the terminus as it allowed space for a large park-and-ride to be added and would serve a large modern village established near Galashiels.

Passenger trains on the Waverley Route returned for the first time in forty-six years on 6 September 2015, when the ScotRail timetable came into full use. An official opening ceremony was led by Her Majesty the Queen on the 9th of that month, who travelled onboard a special steam-hauled excursion from Edinburgh Waverley to Tweedbank, hauled by LNER A4 No. 60009 *Union of South Africa.* The Gresley Pacific was a very appropriate choice, especially as the class was sometimes seen on the Waverley Route in its swansong years. Numerous charter trains would follow on the Borders Railway during the next few years, often steam-hauled, with A3 No. 60103 *Flying Scotsman* also being seen. A3s were one of the most regular classes on the route in BR days. The lack of a run-round loop at Tweedbank means steam and diesel always have to top and tail now.

Being constructed on a tight budget, the Borders Railway is largely single-track for its 30-mile length, but with three dynamic loops giving it a total of 9½ miles of double track for trains to pass at speed. In many locations the single line is positioned along the middle of the former trackbed and overbridges were built to single-track width. This will pose major problems if the railway is ever doubled in the future. This lack of futureproofing has drawn criticism, especially after the decision midway through construction to significantly cut the length of double-track sections originally planned. Generally the ScotRail service is half-hourly, but only one train per hour stops at Stow each way, apart from at peak times.

The reopened Waverley Route has been a major success socially and environmentally for south-east Scotland. Passenger numbers have vastly exceeded expectations, with more than four million travellers in the first three years. It has been a victim of its own success as well though, with overcrowding often being reported, particularly with two-car Class 158s. 158s make up most services but increased usage of the three-car 170s is expected on the back of the central belt electrification, which will help alleviate this.

The biggest concern has been the overall performance of the trains, with delays frequent due to the constraints of single-line working. It was reported that during the first two years almost 1,200 services were cancelled and more than 4,000 journeys were delayed by at least five minutes. These were often put down to signalling problems and staff shortages. As well as this, certain ScotRail services can be cancelled when charter trains run, as the line does not have the capacity for them to fit within the timetable. There are no sidings at Tweedbank, or anywhere else on the line for that matter, which doesn't help.

Although there has been problems, the most important point is that the Borders community has a railway once again and this time it should be here to stay. And reopening of the entire Waverley Route to Carlisle is not as far-fetched an idea as it once was. Campaigning is gathering more momentum and political support, at least for the line to reach Hawick, which is one of the biggest towns in the region. Freight traffic carrying timber from Kielder Forest has often been suggested (25 per cent of England's timber comes from this area so a huge amount of lorries could be removed from the road). Huge credit is of course due to the many locals who fought long and hard to get the Waverley Route partially reinstated and many of the same people are now pushing for Hawick and Carlisle. The new line has really borne fruit for the economy and hopefully this will prompt the government to take other line reopenings more seriously.

A feature of the reopened Waverley Route is some of the original infrastructure still present. The disused station building at Gorebridge dates back to 1847, when it was opened by the North British Rly. This shot of a 158 departing for Edinburgh shows how the line was rebuilt as single-track through here, with just one platform as opposed to two.

The Waverley Route to Carlisle was renowned for its formidable gradients, such as the southbound ascent to Falahill Summit – mostly at 1 in 70 – to a height 880 feet above sea level. The rails have now returned and here we see a 158 bound for Tweedbank reaching the summit on 12 October 2018; a day of freezing gale-force winds at this exposed location.

South of Falahill, the Borders Railway takes a very scenic course, skirting the Gala Water for the rest of the journey. A 158 is pictured heading north near Heriot with autumn colours glowing.

Fountainhall station was not reopened on the Borders Railway, but its building survives, albeit boarded up. On 12 October 2018, Class 158 No. 158712 passes on the 13.29 Tweedbank–Edinburgh. The former level crossing now appears to be a road-rail access point for engineers.

Fushiebridge, Tynehead and Heriot stations were also not reopened, meaning the next one south of Gorebridge is at Stow. It retains its original building (which appears to be in private use) and twin platforms, being on one of three short double-track sections on the route. On 12 October 2018, a northbound 158 pauses on one of the stopping services.

Unlike most of the other stations, Galashiels had to be relocated slightly further north from its original location due to the site being built on in the years following closure. It is now a simple single-platform design, in a narrow embankment alongside the A7 main road. An un-refurbished First-liveried No. 158733 is seen arriving on 12 May 2017, bound for Edinburgh.

The end of the line at Tweedbank – not an original Waverley Route station, but built along with a large park-and-ride to serve a housing development established in the intervening years. The lengthy island platform exists as intended for additional use by charter trains on the line. With this in mind, the absence of a run-round loop or sidings came as something of a surprise.

While the railway comes to an end at Tweedbank, just behind the buffer stops the old Waverley Route trackbed goes on for miles, in parts as a cycle path. Beyond here lie Melrose, Hawick and Carlisle. Will this famous line one day live again? Just as one chapter in Scotland's railway history comes to an end, another could be about to begin...

Acknowledgements

I would like to thanks my friends and family for supporting me in this latest project, especially my father, David Webster, for the use of his excellent photographs once again. Nick Jones, Norman McNab and Andy Scobie (Network Rail) for photographs and operational information. Lastly, thanks to Connor Stait and everyone at Amberley Publishing for their continued guidance. Unless otherwise noted, all other photographs were taken by the author.

11 August 2019 marks the 125th anniversary of the West Highland Line from Craigendoran to Fort William. For more details, plus other WHL news and history, please visit www.westhighlandline.org.uk

Bibliography

www.scot-rail.co.uk
www.railscot.co.uk

Kay, Peter, *Signalling Atlas and Signal Box Directory*, Third Edition (Wallasey: Signalling Record Society, 2010).
West Highland News Plus (Friends of the West Highland Lines magazine).